Published in 2012 by Stewart, Tabori & Chang
An imprint of ABRAMS

Text copyright © 2012 by Wendy Bernard
Photographs copyright © 2012 by Joe Budd

Library of Congress Cataloging-in-Publication Data

Bernard, Wendy.
Custom knits accessories : unleash your inner designer with improvisational techniques for hats, scarves, gloves, socks, and more / by Wendy Bernard ; photographs by Joe Budd.
    p. cm.
"STC Craft/A Melanie Falick book."
ISBN 978-1-58479-955-9
1. Knitting—Patterns. 2. Hats. I. Title.
TT825.B3955 2012
746.43'2—dc23
            2011033821

Editor: Liana Allday
Designer: Anna Christian
Production Manager: Tina Cameron

The text of this book was composed in The Mix and Linotype Univers.

Printed and bound in China.
10 9 8 7 6 5 4 3 2 1

115 West 18th Street
New York, NY 10011
www.abramsbooks.com

custom knits
accessories

Unleash Your Inner Designer with Improvisational Techniques
for Hats, Scarves, Gloves, Socks, and More

Wendy Bernard photographs by Joe Budd
photostyling by Mark Auria

STC Craft | A Melanie Falick Book ✦ New York

CONTENTS

INTRODUCTION

If you're like most knitters (including me), you probably started your knitting career by making a swatch, then a scarf or a hat. I was just a kid when my grandmother taught me how to knit. After a decades-long hiatus, I started again by knitting a cap. Then I knit a scarf. Then I knit a dozen or so felted slippers like a madwoman (and I say this with no disrespect toward knitting madwomen—except you'd probably have to be one to knit a dozen pairs of felted slippers when only one person in your family will wear them). Later, I moved on to my first sweater—a baby sweater—and after that it was adult-size garments, like cardigans, pullovers, and coats. Within just a few years, I was designing my own sweaters, then wrote two books (*Custom Knits* and *Custom Knits 2*) about knitting and customizing top-down garments. So imagine my surprise and delight when my editor suggested I write a book about accessories, giving them the Custom Knits spin. At first I wondered how I'd change my focus; after all, I'd spent years pondering the larger shapes of sweaters. But now I'd get a chance to look at smaller expanses of stitches and revisit the seeds of the knitting bug that my grandmother had first planted in my brain.

One of the first joyful rediscoveries I made about knitting accessories was this: time. How fun it is to design and knit something just a little larger than a swatch that you can sometimes even wear just a few hours after you cast on. Some people spend months, or years, knitting a sweater. They do. I know they do because they tell me. But with accessories knitting, time isn't usually much of a factor. When was the last time you met a knitter who pulled a hat out of her project bag and moaned: "I've been working on this thing for *years* . . ."? As an additional bonus, accessories provide us with endless possibilities for experimenting with stitch patterns without investing too much time. So if you decide to switch out the stitch pattern and don't like the results, you can rip and reknit and it's not a big deal.

Oh, accessories . . . there are so many perks. Not only are they quick, they're also portable. Have you ever tried to take a nearly completed top-down raglan along with you on a plane? Or to the pool? I can't imagine lugging around a huge sweater, but socks?

I could do that. Shoot, I can imagine taking two pairs of socks *and* a cap along with me to the pool . . . With some sunscreen, an umbrella, and something cool to sip, I might be able to finish them all in one day.

Along with the time factor and portability bonus comes another wonderful aspect: yarn, lovely yarn. With accessories, you can use just one coveted hank of hand-painted boutique yarn, or even some leftover yarn, and create a wearable item in no time flat. So not only are accessories a way to justify buying a skein or two of pricey yarn, they'll also help you work through your stash.

I admit, another appealing part of making accessories is that they don't have to fit perfectly. Imagine only taking one measurement—or none—casting on, binding off, and having the item fit! Scarves certainly fall into this carefree category. Mittens? All you need to know is your hand circumference and maybe the length of your longest finger. And if the mitten doesn't come out perfectly, you can relax knowing that you spent relatively little time knitting it.

This isn't to say that I'm not concerned about the finished product. While the fit of an accessory may not be as crucial as the fit of a sweater, we all still want it to come out right. So for this book, I've put lots of emphasis on preplanning, such as showing you how to take accurate measurements, how to recalculate gauge if you want to use a different yarn, and how to flip a stitch pattern to in-the-round (a useful trick since many accessories are worked circularly). Accessory knitting presents the perfect opportunity to try out new techniques and see quick results, so as long as you do some preplanning, you're all set to experiment.

While I was thrilled to focus on this new type of knitting and designing for this book, I can report that I was also thrilled to reach out to two entirely new groups of knitters—beginner knitters who are focusing on smaller projects and those seasoned knitters who mostly love to knit accessories and want to experiment with customizing. It is my hope that this collection will appeal to many types of knitters, especially those who enjoy working without too many barriers and who like to insert their own aesthetic into their knitting. Many accessories are so straightforward that you don't need an elaborate pattern. So in this book, you'll find several of my "recipes" for creating items like berets, socks, and shawls on the fly (and sometimes in just a few steps). If you're interested in trying out designing, these recipes are the perfect way to get started. Add a stitch pattern, play around with the repeats, and who knows? Your designs might find their way into the hands of other knitters, and a new knitwear designer will be born. To help you along, I've also provided charts throughout with common yardage requirements and measurements for different types of accessories, so you'll have all the information you'll ever need to whip up a last-minute gift (or a little something for yourself) without having to scout out a pattern.

I've also included tips and tricks that specifically apply to each type of accessory. Want to add a stitch pattern to a triangular shawl but not sure how to increase in pattern? Find out how to do it on page 24. Want to change a flat stitch pattern from a stitch dictionary to one in the round so you can incorporate it into a sock pattern? On page 22, you'll find steps that show you how to do just that. Want to knit a top-down hat for everyone in the family but with differently shaped crowns? I show you how on page 37. Want to use some yarn from your stash instead of the yarn called for in the pattern, even though they are a different weight and fiber content? Just about everything you need to know is on pages 12 to 15.

And because not everyone wants to design their own patterns or make them up from scratch, I have included a wealth of accessories for you to knit as they are written. As with all patterns in the Custom Knits series, these come with ideas for how to "make it your own" in case you're interested in customizing elements to your liking.

Finally, with every book I write, my sincerest wish is that you will use the information you find here in the way your inner knitter/designer wants: Either follow the directions to a "T" or blend it all with the wild ideas and dreams in your mind. Knitting the Custom Knits way means doing a little preplanning and casting on, then inserting whatever stitches or shapes inspire and move you. In the end, there are no real rules or mistakes that matter, because with every failure there comes understanding and a new beginning. I truly believe that. And, as I always say: If something doesn't work out and you have used anything other than mohair or angora, it'll rip out like a dream . . . .

Wendy.

CHAPTER 1

Preplanning Accessories: Yes, Preplanning

Knitted accessories are typically small in size and quick to make, so it's especially tempting to experiment with designs. Whether you're customizing an existing pattern or making a yarn substitution, there are a few things you'll want to think through before you begin. For instance, if you're swapping yarns, you'll need to figure out how much yarn you need. If you're adding a stitch pattern to an otherwise plain knit, you might need a primer on how to use stitch pattern books. If you want to make an accessory in the round but the pattern is written flat, you'll need to convert the pattern before you begin, and you might also want to know how to create jogless color changes so that your in-the-round stripes will be nice and neat. So in this section, I've devoted some space to figuring out just what you need to do, and preplanning how you're going to get it done.

SUBSTITUTING YARNS: GAUGE AND BEYOND

When it comes to using yarn, knitters are pretty much divided into two camps: those who will search high and low to obtain the exact yarn specified in the pattern right down to the color, and those who rarely use the specified yarn, preferring to use something in their stash or a yarn that they feel puts their personal stamp on the project. Even though accessories tend to be small, you have to be careful when swapping out yarn. Not only does gauge come into play, but the drape of the fabric will also be affected if you substitute a yarn that contains different fibers than the one suggested in the pattern. Other factors that might impact the final result of your garment are how the fiber was processed, your particular style of knitting, and the type of tools you use. Never take anyone else's word: You need to get to know the yarn you choose before you commit to substituting.

Getting to Know Your Yarn

In order to understand your yarn, you need to knit a swatch. Unfortunately, you can't rely on the ball band to tell you your gauge—it's meant to be interpreted as a starting point or a suggestion (i.e., the fabric looks nice when it's knit up at X stitches over Y inches)—but every person's gauge is affected by all sorts of factors. Most people know that going up or down in needle size will affect gauge, but so will changing the type of stitch (for example, cables worked at the suggested needle size will not have the same gauge listed on the ball band). Your mood can also be a contributing factor to gauge (ever knit when you're angry or stressed and find that your stitches are a bit tight?). Even the color of the yarn can affect gauge due to the color dyeing process (for example, a dyed yarn may have a finer or heavier gauge than a natural yarn because the heat or chemicals may compress or "fluff up" the fibers).

Believe it or not, many knitters also find that it's important to test out fibers on a variety of needle types to see how it affects gauge and the overall knitting experience. For instance, if you're knitting silk, you may find that bamboo needles grip the slippery yarn in a way that helps you control it as opposed to metal needles, which can slow down knitting for people who fear they may drop a stitch. The same goes for wool and bamboo (or sometimes even plastic) needles—there are times when the friction between the sticky wool doesn't work well with the matte wood or plastic needles and you'll find that your gauge comes out too tight. If you don't have two needles in the same size that are constructed out of different types of materials, ask a friend or even a nearby yarn store if you can swatch with their needles to see how the yarn behaves.

When it comes down to it, it's all in learning how your hands, tools, stitch pattern, and yarn work together . . . and it's definitely worth taking the time to test, try, and swatch to see what works best.

Skylark Stole (page 87) worked at
a gauge of 3 stitches per inch.

Skylark Stole (page 87) worked at a gauge of 5¼ stitches per inch.

CHANGING GAUGE

Let's say that you have fallen in love with a scarf pattern in a worsted-weight yarn, and the motif has a gauge of 12 stitches over 4 inches, but the yarn you want to use is a smaller gauge. If you want to maintain the "look" and the finished width of the scarf shown in the pattern, you'll need to make a swatch with your new yarn and do a little math. Your swatch should be large enough for you to work at least two repeats of the motif along with the same edging as in the pattern. Once you have finished your swatch, measure each motif and the gauge of the borders. Let's say it's a 12-stitch motif, and after blocking, it measures 2 inches.

Looking at the original pattern, let's say it's 11½ inches across and has a gauge of 5 stitches to the inch, with a 5-stitch Garter border. The pattern calls for an initial cast-on of 58 stitches. If you subtract the two 5-stitch Garter borders, you'll have 48 stitches of actual pattern, or four 12-stitch pattern motifs. Since the gauge is 5 stitches to the inch, those 48 stitches would measure about 9.6 inches across. And if there are 4 motifs in those 9.6 inches, then 9.6 ÷ 4 = 2.4, or roughly 2.5 inches compared to your swatch that measured 2 inches. So how do you make your scarf the same width as the one in the pattern?

If your 12-stitch motifs each measure 2 inches, you could fit 4.8 of them into that space. Round that up to 5 repeats and you will have 10 inches of patterning. From there, decide how many border stitches you want to cast on to bring your final scarf to nearly the exact width as the original scarf. So, when casting on, cast on your first set of border stitches and then cast on 5 sets of 12 (or 60 stitches), then your other set of border stitches. See page 17 for tips on how to estimate yardage requirements in situations like this, to be sure you have enough.

SWATCHING IN THE ROUND

Some knitters find that when they work an item in the round, their gauge changes compared to when they work flat. Why is this so? It's a rare knitter whose gauge remains the same when purling as when knitting. So, if you are working a project in the round, you might be knitting every round; if you switch to working back and forth, where you will purl every other row, your gauge may very well change. So, it is probably a very good idea to make a gauge swatch that is actually in the round rather than flat. You can make a fake circular gauge swatch with two double-pointed needles or a circular needle. Here's how (and note, when making your gauge swatch, that you should work the stitch pattern that is specified in your project):

✦ Cast on enough stitches to give you a large-ish piece of knitting, about 5 or 6 inches wide. Knit one row.

✦ Slide the stitches to the opposite end of the needle without turning the work.

✦ Bring the working yarn behind the work and knit the next row, making sure that you leave the strand in the back very loose.

✦ Continue in this manner, knitting each row until the swatch is square. Bind off or slide the stitches off the needle to make measuring easier.

FIBER CONTENT AND DRAPE

The fiber content of your yarn is one of the most important things to consider when swapping the yarn a pattern suggests for another yarn. For instance, let's say a scarf pattern calls for merino wool and you substitute a rayon blend of the same gauge. Unless you have prior experience with the rayon blend, you may not realize what will happen. You see, even if you work up a swatch and obtain the correct gauge, the rayon will very likely drape so much more than the merino that the scarf will become much longer than you expected. Sure, that won't ruin your day, but if you tried the same substitution with a hat pattern—even if your gauge swatch matched the pattern exactly—your cap would probably turn out too floppy and too large. Why? Because rayon and merino are made from totally different fibers. Rayon is made from cellulose—it's slippery and shimmery and is appreciated for its drape, but it is known to stretch out and lose its shape. Merino, on the other hand, is a protein fiber with excellent "memory"—it can certainly stretch, but it usually springs right back into shape.

So how do you know how your substituted yarn will behave in your completed project? Ultimately, you won't know unless you have worked with it before, and really, it all comes down to a combination of the type of fiber—where the fiber came from, how it was processed, and whether the yarn is formed as a tube, a chain, plied, etc.—as well as how you knit it and the tools that you use. The chart below will give you some direction when substituting one fiber for another. When referring to the chart, know that factors such as gauge and stitch pattern will also affect your project's drape.

To be specific, let's say you want to work the Sangria Shawlette on page 83, but you want to use a lightweight cotton instead of the merino called for in the project. You might be surprised to discover that your finished shawlette won't block out as evenly as you want it to and that the lace pattern is too compact. This is because cotton yarns don't have very much stretch and therefore won't spread out while blocking like the merino will. Wools have much more stretch and take well to blocking, which is why people who knit lace usually prefer these fibers. If you want to use cotton for a lace pattern, you absolutely can, but it will only work if you go up a couple needle sizes. That way, you will be able to see the lace pattern better and you won't have to rely on blocking and re-blocking to reveal it.

TYPICAL FIBER BEHAVIOR

FIBER	FABRIC DRAPE	FABRIC STRETCH	BLOCKING HOLD
Hemp, Linen	Hardly any	Some	Good
Cotton	Some	Some	May not last
Bamboo, Corn, Modal, Rayon, Seacell, Soy	Lots	Lots	Good
Silk	Some	Some	Good
Angora, Cashmere, Mohair, Wool	Some	Some	Good
Alpaca	Lots	Lots	Good

Using Stash and Odd-Ball Yarn

Talk to just about anyone who knits and they'll tell you that not only do they have extra yarn on hand, but they rarely throw out the half-used stuff either. Of course, we all know this accumulation of yarn is called a stash and for the most part, knitters are proud to have one. You will, however, come in contact with those who have rooms full of yarn. I secretly harbor a little bit of envy for these folks, but truth be told, having that much yarn must be a burden of sorts. Imagine it: All that yarn—hundreds of skeins—looking at you, saying, "Knit me! Knit me!", which in reality could take years to accomplish.

Whether you are a Major Stasher or a minor stasher, this section is devoted to how to use up those balls of yarn we've all got tucked away. Couldn't we all stand to take a look at what we have in our stash, unused bits and odd balls alike, to see if there's an opportunity to use it in a project? There are freezing people in China, don't you know! For any and all stash-busting substitutions, consult the yardage approximation chart on pages 18 and 19 to guesstimate if you have enough yarn in your stash to make the project you have in mind.

A SINGLE SKEIN

If you have just one skein of yarn, chances are good that you can put it to use as an accessory. You will find that the heavier the yarn weight (i.e., heavy worsted or bulky), the fewer yards one skein will contain, conversely, the lighter the yarn weight (i.e., lace or fingering), the more yards one skein will contain. So if you have just one hank of lace-weight yarn—which usually come in generous lots of as much as 400 yards—scream with glee over the treetops! You can probably use that one hank of lace-weight yarn for an entire shawl. In some cases, one skein of fingering weight will work up into a pair of socks or some mittens or a cap. Many times, a single skein of worsted-weight yarn will be enough to make a pair of fingerless mittens, and a bulky single skein will yield a smaller item, such as the Modern Turban (shown below).

TWO OR THREE SKEINS

Leg warmers, arm warmers, cowls, and scarves are pretty easy to produce if you have two or three balls of the same weight yarn on hand—particularly if it is of a medium weight. But if you have odd balls or a skein here or there in a similar weight and texture, and you feel like making a multicolored scarf, you'll want to preplan by swatching the various yarns together to see how the textures work when combined. Even though similar textures or fiber contents will result in an item that looks cohesive, it's always fun to experiment when it comes to accessories and see how slightly different yarns work together.

PARTIALLY USED SKEINS— HOW FAR WILL THEY GO?

Knitters are always looking for ways to use half-skeins of yarn instead of allowing them to accumulate. The problem is that you very often don't know how much yarn is left or whether it's enough to complete a project. Let's say, for example, that you want to make a striped scarf using four partially used balls of yarn in similar weights and different colors. The first thing you will want to do is check the approximate yardage requirements chart on pages 18 and 19 to find out how much yarn you'll need to make the scarf size you have in mind.

Once you know how much yarn you'll need, you'll then need to weigh each partial ball on a kitchen scale (or go to the post office and use the scale there) and write down the weight on the inside of the ball band. You might be tempted to try a bathroom scale, but it

The Modern Turban (page 46) is a perfect single-skein project.

won't give you precise measurements down to an ounce or gram (not to mention, yarn rarely comes in pounds). When you weigh the yarn, make sure that you use the same units of measurements used on the ball band (i.e., if the measurements on the label are in ounces, measure in ounces). Then, for each ball, subtract the number of ounces or grams you have left from the original weight to see how many remain. Note that if you've lost the ball band to your partial skein and don't know the original yardage or weight, you can search online and find the information fairly easily—the only requirement is that you have to remember the name of the yarn in order to look it up!

Once you've weighed your yarn, the next step is to do some calculations to find out how many yards you have (and again, do your calculations in the units in which the information is given on the band ... if it's in meters, you can convert the number to yards, or vice versa, at the end). Find the number of yards on the original ball band, and divide it by the number of ounces or grams the yarn ball originally had—this will tell you how many yards you have per ounce or gram. After that, simply take this yards-per-ounce (or gram) number and multiply it by the number of ounces or grams you have left in your partial ball of yarn. This will tell you how many yards are in your partial ball. Repeat this equation for all four odd balls and add up the yardage for each one to find out if you have the total number of yards required to finish your scarf.

Here's an example to show you how the calculations are done: Let's say you have an odd ball of worsted weight yarn that originally came in a 250-yard/4-ounce skein, and it now weighs 2.5 ounces. Divide the total length (yards) by the ounces: 250 yards ÷ 4 ounces = 62.5 yards per ounce. So, we now know that each ounce yields 62.5 yards. Using the new weight of 2.5 ounces, multiply it by the yards per ounce to find out how many yards you have on hand: 62.5 x 2.5 = 156.25 yards remaining.

Assume you weighed all the other balls you want to use and you have a combined total of 382 yards. Looking at the chart on pages 18 and 19, you'll find that a 10" x 60" scarf in a worsted gauge takes about 500 yards, but a 6" x 40" scarf in the same gauge takes about 200 yards. Since you only have 382 yards, you could cast on for a scarf approximately 6 inches wide and know that you'll be able to knit at least 40 inches before you run out, and very likely have enough yarn to add a multicolored fringe.

Estimating How Much Yarn You Need

In each pattern in this book, I tell you how much yarn you need—but only if you use the specified yarn at the required gauge. Since I like to encourage knitters to customize, it's important to discuss ways to estimate how much yarn you'll need. Beyond going to your local yarn shop for professional advice or asking others who've made similar garments how much yarn they used, there is a fairly reliable method to calculate yarn requirements based on a pattern schematic. (Note that if you are designing your own accessory or changing the width or length of a particular pattern, you may need to draw your own schematic, which you can then use to calculate yarn requirements.)

Let's say you want to make a pair of Stockinette-stitch leg warmers that are 15 inches long and 13 inches in circumference and your gauge is 5 rows per inch. First, picture the leg warmers laid flat and opened up, next to one another; this would be a 15-inch-long rectangle that is 26 inches wide. Multiply the length of the leg warmers by the 5 rows per inch and that will give you a total number of rows for the rectangle (15" x 5 rows per inch = 75 rows). As a rule of thumb, one row of Stockinette stitch takes a length of yarn approximately 3 times the width of the piece you are knitting. So, if you think of the rectangle as if it were one whole piece of knitting, each 26-inch-wide row will use 78 inches of yarn (26 x 3). You can then multiply 78 inches of yarn by 75 rows for the rectangle

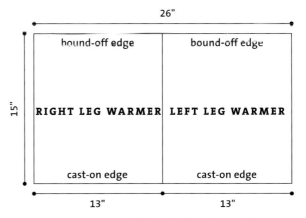

Note: Leg warmers will be worked in the round, but are pictured here as if they are worked flat, for the purpose of illustrating the calculations.

and you'll get 5,850 inches of yarn. Divide that by 36 to find out yardage, and you'll arrive at 162.5 yards for the leg warmers. As a precaution, add another 10 percent for some "padding" when you shop for your yarn.

If you are making your leg warmers with a stitch pattern, make a gauge swatch and measure its width. Then, carefully unravel one row and measure it to find out how many inches of yarn it took to create that row. Say your gauge swatch in ribbing is 4 inches wide, and one unraveled row measures 16 inches. Divide 16 inches of the yarn by the width of the swatch (16 ÷ 4) and you'll find that one row of your ribbing was almost 4 times the width of the swatch. Now you can use that number to determine how much yarn you will require for the ribbed leg warmers.

APPROXIMATE YARDAGE REQUIREMENTS

Note that these measurements are approximations and assume you are using Stockinette stitch. Cables, colorwork, and ribbing take more yarn, as do other textured styles of stitchwork.

BERET	YOUTH	WOMEN'S MEDIUM	WOMEN'S LARGE/MEN'S MEDIUM
4 sts/inch (2.5 cm)	125 (115) yards (meters)	150 (137) yards (meters)	175 (160) yards (meters)
5	150 (137)	185 (169)	225 (206)
6	225 (206)	275 (252)	325 (297)
7	250 (229)	290 (265)	350 (320)
CAP			
4 sts/inch (2.5 cm)	125 (115) yards (meters)	150 (137) yards (meters)	200 (183) yards (meters)
5	150 (137)	200 (183)	250 (229)
6	225 (206)	275 (252)	325 (297)
7	250 (229)	300 (275)	350 (320)
SLOUCH CAP (a cap that is about 2 inches longer than a regular cap)			
4 sts/inch (2.5 cm)	180 (165) yards (meters)	225 (206) yards (meters)	240 (220) yards (meters)
5	240 (220)	270 (247)	300 (275)
6	330 (302)	370 (339)	420 (384)
7	360 (329)	390 (357)	450 (412)

Note that if you want to use cables, it would be best to knit a full repeat of the cable pattern and measure the row where the cable crosses because that is the spot where you'd be using the most yarn.

This method of calculating yarn requirements works for just about any accessory. The only trick is to picture the item laid out flat—it might help to draw your own "flat" schematic so that you can visualize the piece and jot down your calculations.

Beyond using mathematical equations to figure out how much yarn your project will require, you can always use the Approximate Yardage Requirements below.

SCARF	6" x 40"	10" x 60"	
4 sts/inch (2.5 cm)	170 (156) yards (meters)	400 (366) yards (meters)	
5	200 (183)	500 (457)	
6	300 (275)	700 (640)	
7	325 (297)	750 (686)	

FINGERLESS GLOVES	YOUTH	WOMEN'S MEDIUM	WOMEN'S LARGE/MEN'S MEDIUM
4 sts/inch (2.5 cm)	70 (64) yards (meters)	90 (83) yards (meters)	135 (124) yards (meters)
5	80 (73)	120 (110)	160 (147)
6	125 (115)	175 (160)	225 (206)
7	135 (124)	190 (174)	250 (229)

MITTENS			
4 sts/inch (2.5 cm)	80 (73) yards (meters)	100 (92) yards (meters)	150 (137) yards (meters)
5	100 (92)	130 (119)	175 (160)
6	140 (128)	190 (174)	250 (229)
7	150 (137)	200 (183)	275 (252)

SOCKS (above-ankle)			WOMEN'S LARGE	MEN'S MEDIUM
5 sts/inch (2.5 cm)	140 (128) yards (meters)	225 (206) yards (meters)	250 (229) yards (meters)	325 (297) yards (meters)
6	200 (183)	325 (297)	350 (320)	450 (412)
7	225 (206)	350 (320)	400 (366)	550 (503)

SUBSTITUTING STITCH PATTERNS, EDGINGS, AND COLORWORK

Part of the fun of knitting is using your imagination to go beyond what the printed pattern tells you to do. You don't have to design a pattern from scratch—it's easy to swap out one ribbing for another on a pair of leg warmers, or add a panel of lace or some colorwork to an otherwise plain pair of mittens. This section will get you started.

Using Stitch Dictionaries

If you want to experiment by adding various stitch patterns to your knitting and you haven't yet bought or borrowed a stitch dictionary, now is the time to do so. Stitch dictionaries are compilations of many different stitch patterns that people have created over the years. Usually, they offer a photo of the knitted stitch pattern swatch along with written instructions, and sometimes even charts. But best of all, when you flip through a stitch dictionary you can begin to see how each stitch pattern has its own personality, and you can begin to imagine how to combine them for endless possibilities. But watch out— they're addictive. Before too long you'll find yourself reading stitch dictionaries the same way you would a juicy novel.

Knitters of all skill levels can use patterns from stitch dictionaries and incorporate them into their own knitting designs. And yes, I mean all skill levels. If you're a beginner or someone who has only done "plain knitting," you might feel daunted by the prospect of incorporating a stitch pattern into an existing accessory pattern, but really, there's not much to fear. To make most stitch patterns, you only need to know how to do a handful of tasks: Knit, purl, yarn over, increase, decrease, and use a cable needle. You also need to understand how to read the instructions or follow a chart. Other than that, you'll need some knitting needles (of course), some stitch markers, and maybe a pencil and piece of paper or sticky note to keep track of

your place in the instructions. Once you've gathered these tools and amassed your know-how, you're ready to go!

And when I say "ready to go," I mean: Get ready to swatch. If you are going to test out a new stitch pattern, or even make a stitch pattern you've done many times before but with a new yarn, then it's necessary to take your needles and yarn for a test drive. It's impossible to just look at a stitch pattern and truly know how it will look and behave with any given yarn without trying it out first. Not to mention, if you want to make a headband or a scarf using a particular stitch pattern, how will you know how many stitches to cast on? Which reminds me: When you're testing out a stitch pattern, if the pattern calls for a multiple of 5 stitches for one repeat, don't just cast on 5 stitches. Cast on at least four or five repeats plus a few extra stitches on either side of the swatch so you can measure it properly (that's about 20 to 25 stitches, sometimes more for finer yarn, not including edgings). Once you have worked enough to make your swatch roughly square, bind off and block your swatch according to the manufacturer's recommendations. (Even simple stitch patterns like Stockinette should be blocked.)

Once the swatch is dry, it's time to check the gauge. Your main goal here is to figure out how many times you need the stitch pattern to repeat to achieve the width or length that you desire. In the case of a scarf, which is usually worked flat, all you need to do is decide how wide you want it to be, keeping in mind the additional width

Tipsy Pashmina (page 96)
is an example of an elaborate
stitch pattern worked into
a simple scarf.

a border will add, and cast on the appropriate number of stitches (the number of pattern stitches plus the border stitches on each side). Hats are trickier because no matter what you do, you will have to figure out how to increase in pattern, as is the case when working a cap from the top down (see tips for doing this on page 24).

Another challenge is that most stitch dictionaries provide instructions for knitting flat, but many knitted accessories are worked in the round—mittens, socks, gloves, caps, cowls, and infinity scarves, to name a few. So if you want to use a stitch dictionary and avoid sewing your project, knowing the basics of how to change a flat pattern to an in-the-round one is a great idea.

CONVERTING STITCH PATTERNS TO IN-THE-ROUND

To show you how to convert a stitch pattern to in-the-round, I've used the Spiral Columns stitch pattern that appears in the Lipstick Leg Warmers pattern (shown below).

In the "worked flat" stitch pattern at right, you'll see that it has a multiple of 10 stitches, and that there are 4 stitches to be worked before or after working the repeats between the asterisks. When you convert a flat stitch pattern to in-the-round, the first thing you need to do is look at the rows of the pattern and the information contained after the asterisk (if the pattern is written out),

or indicated by the brackets and stitch repeat information (if charted). Then, you need to remove the extra stitch(es) on one or both sides of the pattern.

This Spiral Columns Pattern was a straightforward conversion. Even though there were stitches to be worked before or after the asterisk, all I had to do to convert it to in-the-round was remove those first or last 4 stitches. Then I had to convert the wrong-side rows to rounds. See the stitch patterns side by side at right.

Things are a little more complicated if the edge stitches vary in number. For example, let's say you see a "K1" before the asterisk on one right-side row and then a "K4" on the next right-side row. If you were to simply work the stitches that appear in the asterisks, your pattern wouldn't line up correctly. Instead, take a look at the varying number of stitches that appear before the asterisk. If, on the first right-side row (Row 1), there is a "K1" before the asterisk, and on the second right-side row (Row 3), there is a "K4" before the asterisk, subtract the "K1" from the second "K4" and work only three knit stitches at the beginning of the appropriate round (Rnd 3). If you are confused about where the pattern begins and ends, it may help to look at the pattern visually. Get some graph paper and chart out a couple repeats of the pattern. Draw a line on either side of the pattern repeat and eliminate the stitches that are not needed.

The stitch pattern on the Lipstick Leg warmers (page 134) was converted from a flat pattern to in-the-round.

SPIRAL COLUMNS PATTERN (worked flat)
(multiple of 10 sts + 4; 10-row repeat)

Rows 1 and 3 (RS): P4, *k6, p4; repeat from * to end.

Rows 2 and 4: *K4, p6; repeat from * to last 4 sts, k4.

Row 5: P4, *k2, k2tog, k2, yo, p4; repeat from * to end.

Row 6: *K4, p1-tbl, p5; repeat from * to last 4 sts, k4.

Row 7: P4, *k1, k2tog, k2, yo, k1, p4; repeat from * to end.

Row 8: *K4, p1, p1-tbl, p4; repeat from * to last 4 sts, k4.

Row 9: P4, *k2tog, k2, yo, k2, p4; repeat from * to end.

Row 10: *K4, p2, p1-tbl, p3; repeat from * to last 4 sts, k4.

Repeat Rows 1–10 for Spiral Columns Pattern.

SPIRAL COLUMNS PATTERN (worked in the round)
(multiple of 10 sts; 10-round repeat)

Rnds 1-4: *K6, p4; repeat from * to end.

Rnd 5: *K2, k2tog, k2, yo, p4; repeat from * to end.

Rnd 6: *K5, k1-tbl, p4; repeat from * to end.

Rnd 7: *K1, k2tog, k2, yo, k1, p4; repeat from * to end.

Rnd 8: *K4, k1-tbl, k1, p4; repeat from * to end.

Rnd 9: *K2tog, k2, yo, k2, p4; repeat from * to end.

Rnd 10: *K3, k1-tbl, k2, p4; repeat from * to end.

Repeat Rnds 1–10 for Spiral Columns Pattern.

SPIRAL COLUMNS PATTERN
(worked flat)

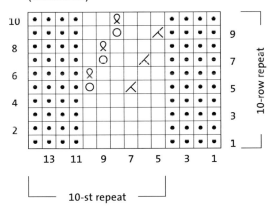

SPIRAL COLUMNS PATTERN
(worked in the round)

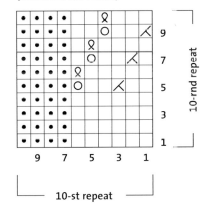

KEY

☐ Knit on RS, purl on WS

• Purl on RS, knit on WS

O Yo

⟋ K2tog

Ω K1-tbl on RS, p1-tbl on WS

Once you've removed the edge stitches, you need to convert your stitch pattern so that each right-side row becomes an odd-numbered round, and each wrong-side row becomes an even-numbered round. This assumes that the stitch pattern begins with a right-side row; if it begins with a wrong-side row, then all your formerly wrong-side rows will become odd-numbered rounds, and all your formerly right-side rows will become even-numbered rounds. So on every other round (the rounds that you converted from wrong-side rows), you'll need to work "inside-out," since the stitches that you formerly worked on wrong-side rows will now be worked on right-side rounds; they have to be worked in reverse so that the knits become purls and the purls become knits (see the Cheat Sheet for Converting Flat to Round, at right, for help converting other stitches, too). If you happen to have chosen a pattern that has slipped stitches on wrong-side rows, be aware that you may need to slip the stitches with the yarn in front instead of in back, or vice versa. Also note that all rounds in charts will now be read from right to left on every round instead of going back and forth as you would with flat knitting.

If your chosen pattern isn't symmetrical, travels in one direction only, or is offset to the left or to the right, you'll want to pause for a second and rethink your wrong-side rows. The wrong-side rows will no longer be worked from left to right, but instead from right to left. So if you want the motif to travel in the intended direction, you not only need to change your knits to purls and purls to knits—you also need to change the wrong-side rows so that they are backwards.

Whatever the case, this conversion can sometimes be tricky, so get out your graph paper and a pencil so that you can write out everything (and chart it, too, if it helps), turning the wrong-side rows around as you write them. Then you can work a swatch with your revised in-the-round instructions to make sure you haven't missed anything.

Shaping in Pattern

If you are making a stole or a scarf that doesn't have shaping, you'll never have to worry about adding stitches and marring your motif. But when you are making shaped accessories like hats or triangular shawls, you will be increasing at the same time you are working your stitch pattern, and there are a few strategies for how to retain

CHEAT SHEET FOR CONVERTING FLAT TO ROUND

When you convert a stitch pattern from flat to in the round, refer to this chart to see how stitches appear on the right side and wrong side.

RIGHT SIDE		WRONG SIDE
Knit	☐	Purl
Purl	⊡	Knit
Yo	⦾	Yo
K1-tbl	⍉	P1-tbl
M1 knitwise	⍉	M1 purlwise
M1 purlwise	⍉	M1 knitwise
K2tog	⍂	P2tog
Ssk	⍁	Ssp
P2tog	⍈	K2tog
K2tog, yo	⦾⍂	Yo, p2tog
Ssk, yo	⦾⍁	Yo, ssp
Wyib		Wyif
Wyif		Wyib

the look of the motif. One strategy is to look for stitch patterns where the fun stuff happens on the right-side rows of the pattern and not on the wrong-side rows so that you can just purl across the wrong side of the item (or if you're working in the round, you'll just knit every other round). It's also a good idea to pay attention to the number of stitches in a pattern repeat (i.e., the fewer stitches in the repeat, the fewer rows or rounds you will have to work before you incorporate or take away the entire repeat . . . but more on that in a moment).

When working with a shaped garment that has a stitch pattern or motif, the easiest way to avoid the problem of shaping within the confines of a stitch pattern is pretty obvious: Don't include a stitch pattern where there will be shaping. For example, some designers will shape the crown of a hat entirely in Stockinette or Garter stitch to avoid dealing with increasing or decreasing in pattern—In these cases, the stitch pattern appears only in the portion of the hat between the brim and the crown. I designed Patsy's Bonnet (shown below) this way, which I would normally consider a cop-out, but in Patsy's case, I liked the effect, so I got lucky. Sometimes, I find that it looks odd for caps to have bold patterns in the main portion and just Stockinette for the crown shaping—kind of like there was no planning involved—so always consider, when shaping, what the overall effect of including or omitting the stitch pattern will be and if your choice will look out of place.

If you do want to incorporate stitch patterns into your shaped accessories, the simplest way to do it is to work a pattern only as long as there are enough available stitches to make a full pattern repeat. In other words, if you are making a neck-down triangular shawl—one that uses increases to shape it—and want to incorporate an 11-stitch lace motif on either side of the center, the easiest way to go about it is to wait until there are at least 11 stitches to work with before starting the lace pattern.

In Patsy's Bonnet (page 50), the stitch pattern appears between the brim and the crown, while the shaping is done in Garter stitch.

The wavy look of the
Cheshire Scarf (page 73)
is created by using two
different needle sizes.

This means that as you add stitches, you will work a "background" stitch. The "background" of a pattern is the type of stitch that appears between elements of the motif. So if you are going to be working a lace pattern, and at least portions (if not all stitches) of wrong-side rows within the pattern are supposed to be knit, then you would be working the lace pattern on a background of Garter stitch. Similarly, if at least portions of wrong-side rows are to be purled, you would be working the lace on a background of Stockinette stitch. You can usually tell by looking at the stitch pattern whether it is worked mostly over Garter stitch or Stockinette stitch. If your pattern is worked over a background of Garter stitch, then you might want to work all your stitches in Garter stitch until you have enough available "background" stitches to make a full pattern repeat; or work those stitches in Stockinette stitch if your pattern is worked over a background of Stockinette stitch. Then when you have enough stitches to make a full pattern repeat, on the next right-side row, simply continue working the stitch pattern on those available stitches.

Here's an example: To make a simple triangular shawl with a center stitch like the one I describe on page 24, you start with a small number of stitches, mark a center stitch and work the shawl in rows, increasing at each edge and at each side of the center stitch. In order to incorporate a leafy motif that has a stitch pattern repeat of 11 stitches on either side of the center stitch, decide what type of stitch will be the leafy motif's background—Stockinette stitch will work well in this case—and work the shawl in rows in Stockinette stitch, increasing on right-side rows at the edges and at either side of the center stitch until there are at least 11 stitches to work with on each side, not including the first 2 stitches (they are for increasing) and the center 4 stitches (also for increasing). So, before you start your 11-stitch lace pattern, you will work your shawl plain (until you have 15 stitches on each side of the shawl, or at least 30 stitches total). As you work your motif on those 11 stitches on each side, and while adding stitches at the increase points and working those added stitches in Stockinette stitch, incorporate another repeat or multiple of that motif as another 11 stitches become available on each side, and so on.

A more complicated strategy is to chart out the stitch pattern and, as stitches become available or are taken away, work a partial repeat of the multiple only and allow the stitch pattern to grow and become fully visible as you progress. The benefit of spending extra time to chart out your pattern is that you will have less "white space" or background stitches. You'll have an accessory that has an allover pattern rather than sections of lace or texture next to plain knitting.

The last solution—though hardly the most accurate—is to change needle sizes for shaping in pattern rather than changing the stitch count. This isn't my favorite strategy because if you're working a texture or stitch pattern, the size and ratio of stitches to rounds/rows changes and distorts. Not only that, there is always the risk that you will pick up the wrong size needle, work happily, and not notice the mistake until it's too late! In order to make the shaping noticeable enough, you'd have to have a selection of different-size needles on hand and make sure that the shaping is spot-on after blocking. The Cheshire Scarf (shown at left) utilizes this technique by switching to smaller needles in the ribbed sections so that they pull in even more and create a wavy look.

Substituting Edges:
Keeping Your Edges From Rolling

My grandmother taught me the basics when I was a little girl. You know, knit the right-side rows and purl the wrong-side rows. But, much later, when I knit a Stockinette-stitch scarf for a boyfriend in high school—one that must have been 10 feet long—I marveled at how it instantly rolled itself into a snake. No matter what I did, or how many times I wet-blocked it, it would continue to roll up on itself. Looking back, it's no wonder I couldn't figure out how to make it stop—the Internet wasn't yet available and ripe for investigation, and I don't think I ever bothered to call up my grandmother and ask her how to fix my problem. She made mittens, slippers, and afghans using textured stitches, so none of what she knit rolled like my Stockinette stitch scarves did.

Knitters have all sorts of explanations as to why Stockinette stitch rolls the way it does, and many say that it's because one side of the knitting has longer stitches than the other, but I'm not so sure. All I know is that if you knit one side and purl the other, it will always roll, and the only way to make it stop is to put a border around it. Non-rolling stitches—such as Moss stitch, Seed stitch, Garter stitch, and pretty much any kind of ribbing—can be used to border any accessory, though they are most commonly needed on flat accessories, like a scarf or a stole. To do so, simply cast on the required number and multiple of stitches plus however many stitches you want to keep as a border and work several rows in any nonrolling stitch; then work the first and last inch of each row in the same nonrolling pattern. Sure enough, your scarf or stole will lay nice and flat. If you are planning to knit a lace pattern in a fine yarn that will be blocked out later, knitting the 2 or 3 stitches at the beginning and end of every row will give you a Garter stitch border, which will almost always do the trick. But I say almost always because you can't be sure it will work until you do a swatch and see how the yarn behaves.

Some people claim that you can keep Stockinette stitch from curling if you slip the first stitch of every row as if to purl, but I wouldn't bet on it. Some yarns that have a nice firm twist might curl up and defy this method, and unfortunately, you'd have to make a hefty swatch using this technique just to find out if it will work with your yarn. So in my opinion, it's best to avoid.

If you have completed an accessory like a stole or scarf or shawl and it is rolling, another method is to add a decorative edging and knit it onto the selvedge edges—there are whole stitch books that are devoted to the subject of adding attractive and functional borders.

There will be times when you actually want edges to roll, like on a simple cap, so if you omit ribbing at the bottom, the edges will roll. If you just want a little bit of roll, you can create a "dam" in your knitting so that it doesn't completely roll up. If you're working a cap top down and in the round, you can add a dam about an inch before you want to bind off. When you reach that point, simply purl a couple rounds, then work several rounds of Stockinette stitch and bind off. Those rounds of Reverse Stockinette stitch (the dam) will stop the cap from rolling further. If you are working from the brim up toward the crown, just cast on and work in Stockinette stitch for several rounds, purl a couple rounds, then change back to Stockinette or the stitch of your choice and carry on up toward the crown.

Substituting or Adding Colorwork: Splashes of Color Are Your Friends

Accessories are perfect occasions for using colorwork, be they stripes, Fair Isle, or multicolored yarns, such as variegated, hand-painted, and self-striping or self-patterning. You may not want all of that color in a sweater, but on mittens or a hat . . . why not?

STRIPES

If you have odd balls of yarn sitting around, striped accessories are a great way to use them up, but it can be a bit of challenge to come up with a plan for the stripes. Do you want them to be orderly like the ones on the Canoodle Arm Warmers (shown at right)? Or do you want them to be semi-orderly like the ones on the Sparkle Ticking Wrap on page 91? Or totally random? Random is fun, but to be totally random requires that you let your hair down a little (well, actually, a lot). And for us knitters who like to take control of our knitting, it can be challenging to let go of our analytical sides.

For those knitters who want control but could use a little guidance, try utilizing a random stripe generator, which you can find on the Internet. These random stripe generators are programs that, after you input your variables—number of colors, number of rows allowed per color, and your colors—create a sequence of colors and random numbers of stripes for you to follow. Many of them allow you to "refresh" the generated sequence until you are satisfied with the way it looks and then print out the sequence for safekeeping.

If you are looking for a stripe sequence idea and don't want to use an online tool, you can put some simple arithmetic to work and come up with a stripe sequence using the Fibonacci progression, where each number is added to the number before it to get the next number in the series. This is how it works: Start with one stripe of one color, then add that number to itself to come up with two, then one plus two to get three stripes, then three plus two to get five stripes, and so on. At some point, you will want to stop the sequence and repeat it, otherwise the stripes will become too wide. Depending upon the number of colors, it may not be that obvious that you're repeating the same sequence over and over.

The Canoodle Arm
Warmers (page 127)
are a perfect way
to use up odd balls
of yarn.

HIDING "JOGS" WHEN WORKING IN THE ROUND

Avoiding hand sewing is my own personal national pastime. And although I typically stay away from lots of stripes, I do like to use them judiciously, where they won't draw attention to certain body parts. Stripes can be tricky when worked in the round—you are basically creating a spiral, so when you change colors (for stripes, in particular), you can see a "jog," or a spot where the stripe or color change isn't nice and straight. There are a couple methods to avoid this color jog, if you are so inclined.

Method 1: Knitting Two Colors Together

Whenever you are working in the round and using stripes, be sure to make your color change in a place where you have the best chance to hide it, like the inside of the ankle, the inner part of an arm warmer or leg warmer, or the palm side of a mitten or glove. Then, when it is time to make a color change, knit the first stitch of the next round with both colors—the old one and the new one—then drop the old one and continue knitting. Once you have knit several rounds or even after you have completed knitting the garment, use the end of a needle to tease out the yarn ends a little bit so that the old color is on the right-hand side of the knit-stitch "V" and the new color is to the left. This makes the color change look like it is in the middle of a stitch, instead of a jog.

Method 2: Lifting the Stitch from the Round Below

Another method is to go ahead and start a new color (just drop the old color behind the work), and when you finish one round with the new color, lift the stitch from the round below (the old color) and place it on the left-hand needle. Knit the first stitch of the following round together with the one you placed on the needle.

USING FAIR ISLE OR INTARSIA

Fair Isle (or stranded knitting) and intarsia are two types of colorwork that are great in knitted accessories. Fair Isle usually features small patterns and uses the same colors repeatedly for the length of a row. It works best for in-the-round projects because you'll always have the right side facing you. With intarsia, unlike Fair Isle, the yarn is never carried across the back of the fabric, and it is characterized by shapes of color that create pictures. Intarsia is generally worked back and forth, and although there is a fancy method out there to allow you to use intarsia in the round, it'll make your life much easier to use Fair Isle for in the round and intarsia for flat patterns.

When adding colorwork to your knits, treat it the same way you would when working with a stitch dictionary. Just look at the multiple of stitches required for the colorwork motif and compare it to the number of available stitches you have in your project; then adjust, if needed. If the color pattern repeat is large and has a distinct center, you might consider aligning it with the center of the project.

Choosing Colors for Colorwork

For me, choosing colors is both the most fun and the most daunting aspect of colorwork. I was once told to put all the colors you plan on using in a basket or a bowl in the approximate order and amount in which you plan to use them. Then take a look and see if the colors you want to be most prominent are coming through. You may need to rearrange until you're happy, and if you can't seem to get it right, try swapping the light and the dark or the warm and the cool until the balance of color seems right.

If you want to avoid choosing colors altogether, you can always use nifty self-striping or self-patterning yarns. These have coloration that is preprogrammed by a computer so that, when you knit it up at the right gauge, it appears as if you intentionally knit a striped or Fair Isle item when it's really just the yarn doing the work for you. Variegated yarns are another great way to sidestep fancy colorwork and keep yourself from agonizing over color choices. Not to mention, many beautifully hand-painted yarns are high priced and are therefore more suited to making something smaller, like a pair of gloves or a beautiful stole. If you have odd balls of variegated yarn, they're great for adding stripes in an accessory project. The subtle color changes within the stripes will be eye-catching.

PORTABILITY CHECKLIST

Accessories tend to be small, so you can take them with you and work on them when you have downtime. Here are a few things to keep in mind if you plan on doing just that.

✦ There are a number of knitting bags on the market that have enough room for your everyday essentials as well as your knitting stuff (the project, needles, scissors, etc.). They range from lightweight and relatively inexpensive to large and pricey, and they are a great way to balance your life and your knitting.

✦ Look for a smallish drawstring bag (or sew one for yourself if you have the know-how) for your knitting so you can fit it into your purse or keep it in your car in case an opportunity to knit arises.

✦ You would think that airplanes, trains, and jury duty would be the perfect places to knit, but sometimes our knitting tools are not allowed in these venues. Call ahead and speak to a human before you bring your knitting needles and scissors. Don't rely on what the website says—you might wind up getting your tools confiscated. To play it safe, leave all cutting tools at home (or pack them in checked luggage) and bring plastic or wooden needles (or needles that you wouldn't mind getting taken away from you). Make sure that the circulars you bring are short, and that your tapestry needle is plastic and dull. And if you're really unsure, place your project on some scrap yarn so if you have to remove the needles and hand them over to the "authorities," at least you won't drop all of your stitches.

✦ If you find yourself without a stitch marker, small ponytail holders, plastic rings from water bottles, paperclips, and safety pins can all help in a pinch. Or simply take a short piece of yarn and knot it into a loop.

✦ There are differing attitudes when it comes to knitting in public meeting places, such as in church or in lecture halls. While *we* know that we can listen, interact, and knit at the same time, others may find it distracting or disrespectful. Rather than give knitters a bad name, it can't hurt to check with the organizer to make sure the meeting is knit-friendly.

✦ Instead of taking your whole pattern book along with you, make a photocopy of the pattern pages for out-of-house knitting. It's also a good idea to keep a pencil in your project bag to keep your place or make notes. A sticky note is another good, small tool that you can move around the pattern to help keep your place as you work a chart or a stitch pattern.

✦ For portable knitting, choose projects that are simple and require little concentration. If you insist on lace, insert a lifeline by threading waste yarn through an entire row or round of stitches. That way, if you find yourself seated next to a chatterbox and lose your place in the pattern, it will be easy to rip back to the row where you started.

CHAPTER 2

Top It Off: Hats, Caps, Bonnets, and Turbans

Hats are probably the second most knitted accessory right behind scarves. They can be worked flat, in the round, top to bottom, bottom to top, and even sideways, and they can be as simple or intricate as you want. As an added bonus, head sizes are fairly consistent by age and gender, so "trying on" for fit isn't terribly important—especially useful if you're making a hat as a gift.

CHOOSING A DIRECTION: IT'S ALL ABOUT FLEXIBLITY

When it comes to knitting something quickly—or throwing stitches on the needles and experimenting—a knit cap is the perfect project. Most often, a knit cap is worked from the ribbing up toward the crown and features a series of decreases to close the top, but it can also be worked flat and then seamed up later, or worked in the round from the top down. But what are the benefits of working these different ways?

Truth be told, there are benefits to each method. For instance, sometimes you will want to make your hat from the bottom up working flat, adding an extra stitch on each side of each row and sewing it up later (yes, sewing). But why would you want to work this way? Well, if you are using a stitch pattern from a stitch dictionary, you won't have to do any extra work to figure out how to change the flat stitch pattern to in the round or flip it upside down—you can simply use it as is. Also, since it's a small item, sewing it up will take no time at all. Another reason you might want to work a cap flat is if you want to use a bit of intarsia, which works best on flat-knit objects. So if, for instance, you wanted to make a cap for a child featuring a rabbit centered on the front, working that cap flat and sewing it up later would be the easiest way to go about it.

Another popular option is to make the hat from the bottom up in the round. This method is especially great if you are incorporating a stitch pattern from a stitch dictionary into your hat design and want to avoid changing the orientation of the stitch pattern from bottom up to top down (though you would still have to convert it to working in the round—see page 22). The downside of bottom-up knitting is that it's difficult to try on as you go, so you'll have to rely on measurements a bit more to figure out when to decrease for the crown.

For optimal control over the way your hat will fit, it's best to work from the top down in the round so that you can try on the hat as you knit. This is why most, but not all, of the caps in this book are worked from the top down. Another benefit of top-down hats is that it's easier to tell whether or not you'll run out of yarn, so you can make the decision to create a shorter cap, or change the yarn at the brim and finish it with a contrasting color instead.

No matter your favorite method, it's best to be flexible when knitting and designing a cap, so whether it is worked from the bottom or from the top—or even side to side working it flat—you'll make the best choice for your finished project and your overall knitting enjoyment.

The Sand Dollar Slouch (page 58) is worked top down, so you can try on as you go for a perfect fit.

Basic Top-Down In-the-Round Hat Formula

Since the universe already abounds with bottom-up cap patterns, in this section, I present a simple formula for making top-down caps and berets without a pattern. You'll need a set of double-pointed needles (dpn), 6 or 8 stitch markers, a 12"- or 16"-long circular needle (optional), and waste yarn (if you're casting on provisionally). Just take some measurements, do some calculations, and you're all set.

1. Knit a gauge swatch.

2. Fill in the blanks below.

Stitches per inch (from your swatch): _____. (A)

Goal head circumference for brim: _____. (Negative ease is required for a close-fitting brim. Subtract an inch or two for best fit. See below for typical head circumferences.) (B)

Caps:

$A \times B \div 8 =$ _____ rounded to a whole number. (C)

Berets:

Goal circumference for largest point of crown: Head circumference + 50% = _____. (D)

$A \times D \div 6 =$ _____ rounded to a whole number. (E)

3. Now that you know your gauge and size, calculate how much yarn you'll need (see page 17).

4. From here on, it's easy. Cap numbers are given first, followed by beret numbers in parentheses; where only one number is given, it applies to both.

Using dpn, CO 8 (6) sts, using a CO of your choice or Provisional CO (see Special Techniques, page 138).

TYPICAL HEAD MEASUREMENTS

Circumference of Head (Subtract up to 2" for a tighter fit.)

	PREEMIE	BABY	TODDLER	CHILD	WOMAN	MAN
	12"	15"	17"	18 – 19"	20"	22"

Approximate Hat Measurements (depth, including edging)

CAP						
	5 ¼"	6"	7 ½"	9"	10 ¾"	12"
SLOUCH CAP						
	6 ¼"	8"	8 ½"	10"	11 ¾"	13"
BERET						
	5 ¾"	6"	6 ½"	7 ¼"	8 ¾"	10"
SLOUCH BERET (Add an extra inch or two for a super-slouchy "Rasta" hat.)						
	6 ½"	8"	8 ½"	9 ¼"	10 ¾"	12"

Rnd 1: K1-f/b into each st—16 (12) sts. Divide sts among 3 needles. Join for working in the rnd; pm for beginning of rnd.

Rnd 2: Knit.

Rnd 3: *K1, k1-f/b; repeat from * to end—24 (18) sts.

Rnd 4: Knit, placing markers after every third st—8 (6) markers, including beginning of rnd marker. *Note: You may wish to use a different color to mark the beginning of the rnd.*

Shape Crown

Note: Change to circ needle if desired to accommodate number of sts on needles (optional).

Cap: *K1-f/b, work to marker, sm; repeat from * to end—32 sts. Knit 1 rnd.

Beret: [K1-f/b (or M1-r if you prefer), work to next marker, k1-f/b (or M1-l if you prefer), sm] 6 times—30 sts. Knit 1 rnd.

Repeat the last 2 rnds until the stitch count per section equals C (E). Work even until the cap/beret measures your desired depth to the beginning of the ribbing (see chart at left for typical depth).

Beret: *K2tog; repeat from * to end. You will have half the stitches you had at the beginning of the rnd.

Cap or Beret: Change to desired rib pattern or hem. *Note: You may have to increase or decrease a few stitches to accommodate the multiples in your chosen rib or hem pattern.* BO all sts loosely in pattern. Thread tail through CO sts or place provisional sts onto 3 dpns and thread tail through live sts. Pull tight and fasten off. Block as desired.

SHAPING THE CROWN IN TOP-DOWN PATTERNS

Depending on how you place your increases, you can achieve a few different crown effects.

Concentric Circles or Circular "Yoke" Style: Evenly place your chosen number of markers, then every other round, increase using either a M1 or a k1-f/b randomly between markers, being careful not to stack the increases. The Sunshine Yoked Beret on page 54 was worked in this manner.

Swirled Effect: On every other round, *M1 or k1-f/b, work to next marker, sm; repeat from * to end.

Wheel or Spoke Effect: For a regular cap, pair the increases, and work them every fourth round instead of every other round: *M1-r, work to marker, M1-l, sm; repeat from * to end. If you want, you can work k1-f/b instead of M1, which will look a little different: *k1-f/b, work to 1 st before marker, k1-f/b, sm; repeat from * to end. For a beret, work these same increases, but work them every other round instead of every fourth round.

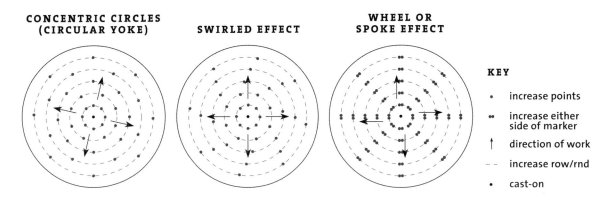

CONCENTRIC CIRCLES (CIRCULAR YOKE) **SWIRLED EFFECT** **WHEEL OR SPOKE EFFECT**

KEY

- • increase points
- •• increase either side of marker
- ↑ direction of work
- - - increase row/rnd
- • cast-on

PATTERN FEATURES
Top-down construction, simple shaping, ribbing.

FINISHED MEASUREMENTS

16" circumference

YARN

Berroco Peruvia Quick (100% Peruvian highland wool; 103 yards / 100 grams): 1 hank #9127 Palomino Blue

NEEDLES

One set of five double-pointed needles (dpn) size US 11 (8 mm)

One 16" (40 cm) long circular (circ) needle size US 11 (8 mm) (optional)

One 16" (40 cm) long circular needle size US 9 (5.5 mm)

Change needle size if necessary to obtain correct gauge.

NOTIONS

Stitch markers

GAUGE

12 sts and 22 rows = 4" (10 cm) in Garter stitch, using larger needles

15 sts and 22 rows = 4" (10 cm) in 4x2 Rib, using smaller needles

CHESHIRE CAP

I recently saw a bulky slouchy hat in a fashion magazine and it looked so cozy and oversized that I just had to create one, putting my spin on it. I'm not usually a big fan of Garter stitch, but worked at this scale, the purl stitches look luscious. Since this cap is worked top down, you can easily adjust its depth for someone who wants a little more or a little less slouch. Pair it with the scarf on page 73 and you have yourself a matching set.

STITCH PATTERN

4x2 Rib

(multiple of 6 sts; 1-rnd repeat)

All Rnds: *K4, p2; repeat from * to end.

NOTE

This Hat is worked from the Crown down to the Brim.

CROWN

Using dpn, CO 8 sts.

Row 1 (RS): *K1-f/b; repeat from * to end—16 sts. Divide sts among 4 needles. Join for working in the rnd, being careful not to twist sts; pm for beginning of rnd.

Rnd 2: Purl.

Rnd 3: *K1, k1-f/b; repeat from * to end—24 sts.

Rnd 4: Purl, placing marker every 3 sts (8 total markers; you may wish to use a different color marker for beginning of rnd).

Shape Crown

Note: Change to circ needle if desired to accommodate number of sts on needles (optional).

Rnd 1: *K1-f/b, knit to next marker, sm; repeat from * to end—32 sts.

Rnd 2: Purl.

Repeat Rnds 1 and 2 until there are 10 sts between markers, ending with Rnd 2—80 sts. Continuing in Garter st (knit 1 rnd, purl 1 rnd), work even for 12 rnds, removing all but beginning-of-rnd marker on first rnd.

Decrease Rnd: Knit, decreasing 10 sts evenly around—70 sts remain. Purl 1 rnd. Repeat Decrease Rnd once—60 sts remain. Purl 1 rnd.

BRIM

Change to smaller needle and 4x2 Rib; work even for 11 rnds. BO all sts in pattern.

FINISHING

Thread CO tail through CO sts. Pull tight and fasten off. Block as desired.

MAKE IT YOUR OWN

You can reduce the amount of slouch by working fewer increases than called for in the pattern. Just count your stitches every now and then and multiply the number on the needles by the stitches per inch—that way, you'll find out what the circumference will be. When the degree of slouch is to your liking, just try it on by either placing your live stitches on waste yarn and pulling it over your head, or placing the stitches on a long circular so you can try it on without the stitches falling off. When you are within 2½ inches of the desired length, decrease enough stitches evenly around to get to 80 stitches, purl one round, then decrease 10 stitches evenly around, followed by another purl round. Then begin the ribbing.

PATTERN FEATURES
Ribbing, stranded (Fair Isle) colorwork, simple shaping.

FINISHED MEASUREMENTS

18 ¼" circumference

YARN

Brown Sheep Company Nature Spun Sport (100% wool; 184 yards / 50 grams): 1 skein each #880 Charcoal (MC), #N03 Grey Heather (A), and #308 Sunburst Gold (B)

NEEDLES

One 16" (40 cm) long circular (circ) needle size US 4 (3.5 mm)

Change needle size if necessary to obtain correct gauge.

NOTIONS

Stitch markers; tapestry needle

GAUGE

28 sts and 30 rnds = 4" (10 cm) in Jacquard Pattern from Chart

JACQUARD SLOUCH

While exploring different hat and cap shapes, this square-yet-squishy shape became one of the ones I found most intriguing. The hat itself is essentially a square, but in order to avoid a super blocky look, I placed some shaping on either side of the crown to soften the contours. For this hat it is important to use a soft yarn with enough drape so you can kind of squish it down and mold it to your head—otherwise, you might look like a blockhead.

STITCH PATTERNS

2x2 Rib
(multiple of 4 sts; 1-rnd repeat)

All Rnds: *K2, p2; repeat from * to end.

Corrugated Rib
(multiple of 4 sts; 1-rnd repeat)

All Rnds: *K2 in A, p2 in MC; repeat from * to end.

NOTE
This Slouch is worked from the Brim to the Crown.

BRIM
Using MC, CO 128 sts. Join for working in the rnd, being careful not to twist sts; pm for beginning of rnd. Begin 2x2 Rib; work even for 2 rnds.

Next Rnd: Change to Corrugated Rib; work even for 9 rnds.

Next Rnd: Change to MC; knit, increasing 10 sts evenly spaced around—138 sts. Change to B; knit 1 rnd. Change to MC; knit 1 rnd.

CROWN
Next Rnd: Change to Jacquard Pattern from Chart; work even until 3 vertical repeats of Chart have been completed. *Note: You may work additional vertical repeats if desired to make piece more slouchy.*

Shape Crown

Next Rnd: Change to MC and St st (knit every rnd); k69, pm, work to end.

Next Rnd: Decrease 4 sts this rnd, then every other rnd 6 times, as follows: [K1, k2tog, knit to 3 sts before marker, ssk, k1] twice—110 sts remain.

FINISHING
Transfer sts between first and second markers to spare needle, removing markers; using Kitchener st (see Special Techniques, page 138), graft halves of Crown together. Block as desired.

JACQUARD PATTERN

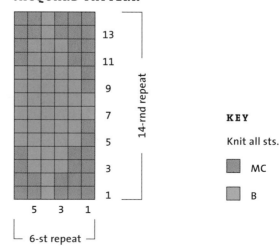

14-rnd repeat

13
11
9
7
5
3
1

5 3 1

6-st repeat

KEY

Knit all sts.

MC

B

MAKE IT YOUR OWN

You can substitute all kinds of colorwork patterns on items like this one, as long as you use the same multiple of stitches (or you can make a slight adjustment to the number of stitches on the needles to incorporate your own colorwork design). The opposite is true as well: Whenever you see a color pattern, know that you can omit it altogether if you want. The variation shown below has the same little stripe and corrugated rib as the original, but that's it—it's essentially the same pattern with most of the colorwork omitted. This variation was made with one skein of Brown Sheep Company Nature Spun Sport in Pepper (#601) and several yards of Charcoal (#880).

FINISHED MEASUREMENTS

17" circumference

YARN

**Spud & Chloë Outer (65% wool /
35% organic cotton; 60 yards /
100 grams): 1 hank #7200
Soapstone**

NEEDLES

**One set of five double-pointed
needles (dpn) or one 16" (40 cm)
long circular (circ) needle size US 11
(8 mm)**

**Change needle size if necessary
to obtain correct gauge.**

NOTIONS

Stitch marker

GAUGE

**12 sts and 18 rows = 4" (10 cm)
in Seed stitch**

MODERN TURBAN

I don't know who originally popularized the turban—
Elizabeth Taylor comes to mind—but truth be told, when
I was waaaay younger, I used to see them plopped atop
the heads of elderly ladies who were probably hiding a
bad hair day. These days, the turban is cropping up in
fashion again, so I decided to take the silhouette and
minimize it into a headband style with just enough fabric
to cover up your ears. Your hairdo? That's for you to
figure out.

STITCH PATTERNS

Seed Stitch worked in the rnd
(odd number of sts; 1-rnd repeat)

Rnd 1: *K1, p1; repeat from * to last st, k1.

Rnd 2: Knit the purl sts and purl the knit sts as they face you.

Repeat Rnd 2 for Seed Stitch worked in the rnd.

Seed Stitch worked back and forth
(even number of stitches)

Row 1: *K1, p1; repeat from * to end.

Row 2: Knit the purl sts and purl the knit sts as they face you.

Repeat Row 2 for Seed Stitch worked back and forth.

TURBAN

CO 51 sts. Join for working in the rnd, being careful not to twist sts; pm for beginning of rnd. Begin Seed st worked in the rnd; work even until piece measures 3½" from the beginning. BO all sts knitwise.

TIE

CO 8 sts. Begin Seed st worked back and forth; work even until piece measures 6½" from the beginning.

BO all sts knitwise, leaving a 12" tail.

FINISHING

Block as desired. Wrap Tie around Turban (see photo). Using tail, sew CO and BO edges of Tie together.

MAKE IT YOUR OWN

This is a perfect pattern for using up stash or odd-ball yarn because it doesn't take much. If you need to substitute yarn and want the dimensions to remain the same, you'll need to make a swatch using Seed stitch. Assuming you want the same dimensions, look at your stitches per inch and multiply one inch's worth of stitches by the finished circumference (17 inches). Note, also, that you might decide to make the circumference larger or smaller depending on how the fiber in your yarn stretches. When working Seed stitch in the round, you will need an odd number of stitches. Work to the length called for in the pattern (3 ½ inches) and bind off. When working the turban tie, repeat the process of reading your swatch and multiplying the number of stitches per inch by the width of the tie in the pattern (2 ¾ inches) to find out how many stitches to cast on. Since you work the tie flat in Seed stitch, this number should be even. This variation was worked with one hank of Plymouth Yarns Royal Llama Silk in #1841, which I worked at a gauge of 4 stitches per inch on size-8 needles, so the cast-on number was 67. Because of the thinner gauge, I made the tie portion 6 inches long instead of 6 ½ inches.

FINISHED MEASUREMENTS

9 ½" from base of Bonnet to top

6" from face to back of head

YARN

Malabrigo Merino Worsted
(100% merino wool; 210 yards /
100 grams): 1 hank #41 Burgundy

NEEDLES

One 24" (60 cm) long circular (circ)
needle size US 7 (4.5 mm)

One set of five double-pointed
needles (dpn) size US 7 (4.5 mm)

Change needle size if necessary to
obtain correct gauge.

NOTIONS

Stitch markers

GAUGE

20 sts and 32 rows = 4" (10 cm)
in Garter Rib

PATSY'S BONNET

I'll be honest: I never thought I'd knit or design a bonnet.
But one day I saw a picture of a mod model from the
'60s wearing one with such charm and panache, I had to
whip up a design of my own. Worked in one piece with
no seaming, you could easily finish this project in a day.
The knitted flowers at the ties add just the right amount
of pizzazz.

STITCH PATTERN

Garter Rib

(multiple of 6 sts + 5; 2-row repeat)

Row 1 (RS): Knit.

Row 2: K4, *p3, k3; repeat from * to last st, k1.

Repeat Rows 1 and 2 for Garter Rib.

NOTES

The Bonnet is worked back and forth, then joined to work in the rnd to shape the back.

If you wish to make a larger Bonnet, simply add sts in multiples of 6. For every 6 sts you add, you will add ⅝" to the length from neck to top of head.

BONNET

CO 95 sts. Knit 1 row. Begin Garter Rib; work even for 6", ending with Row 1. Do not turn. Change to dpns. Join for working in the rnd; pm for beginning of rnd.

Shape Bonnet

Rnd 1: P4, *k2tog, k1, p3; repeat from * to last 7 sts, k2tog, k1, p4—80 sts remain.

Rnd 2: Knit.

Rnd 3: P4, *k2, p3; repeat from * to last 6 sts, k2, p4.

Rnd 4: K4, *k2tog, k3; repeat from * to last 6 sts, k2tog, k4—65 sts remain.

Rnd 5: P2tog, purl to end—64 sts remain.

Rnd 6: Knit, placing marker every 8 sts (8 total markers; you may wish to use a different color marker for beginning of rnd).

Rnd 7: *P2tog, purl to next marker, sm; repeat from * to end—56 sts remain.

Rnd 8: Knit.

Repeat Rnds 7 and 8 until there are 2 sts between markers—16 sts remain.

Next Rnd: *P2tog; repeat from * to end—8 sts remain. Cut yarn, leaving a 12" tail; thread through remaining sts, pull tight and fasten off.

FINISHING

Tie

Using dpns, CO 4 sts. Work I-Cord 40" long (see Special Techniques, page 138). Fold in half to find center point and tack at point where Bonnet is joined to work in the rnd. Sew I-Cord to side edges of back-and-forth rib section.

Flowers

Small Flower (make 2)

CO 36 sts. *K1, BO next 4 sts (1 st left on right-hand needle after BO); repeat from * to end—12 sts remain. Cut yarn, leaving a 12" tail; thread through remaining sts, pull tight and fasten off.

Large Flower (make 1)

CO 70 sts. *K1, BO next 5 sts (1 st left on right-hand needle after BO); repeat from * to end—20 sts remain. Cut yarn, leaving a 12" tail; thread through remaining sts, pull tight and fasten off.

Place one Small Flower over Large Flower and sew together, then sew to one end of Tie. Sew remaining Small Flower to other end of Tie.

MAKE IT YOUR OWN

If you prefer, you can attach little (or big) pom-poms to the ends of the ties instead of flowers. And if you don't like the Garter stitch section in the back of the bonnet (see photo on page 25), you can substitute by knitting all rounds in Stockinette and incorporating the decreases as written.

PATTERN FEATURES
Top-down construction,
simple stitch pattern,
simple shaping.

SIZES
Youth (Woman)

FINISHED MEASUREMENTS
17 ¾ (20 ¼)" circumference

YARN
Koigu Painter's Palette Premium
Merino (KPPPM) (100% merino
wool; 175 yards / 50 grams): 2 hanks
#P509

NEEDLES
One set of five double-pointed
needles (dpn) size US 2 (2.75 mm)

One 20" (50 cm) long circular
(circ) needle size US 2 (2.75 mm)
(optional)

Change needle size if necessary to
obtain correct gauge.

NOTIONS
Stitch markers

GAUGE
28 sts and 48 rnds = 4" (10 cm) in
Stockinette stitch (St st)

SUNSHINE YOKED BERET

This top-down beret features one of my favorite techniques for shaping a cap: I just tell myself that I am going to randomly increase a certain number of stitches each round or every other round (in this case, I increased 8 stitches randomly every other round), and when I'm done with the crown, you can barely detect the increases at all. In order to make the increases truly random, you just need to be relaxed, not letting yourself get too uptight with the increase placements. When you're done, I promise you'll have an unfussy crown that doesn't swirl or twirl. Instead, it just "is."

STITCH PATTERN

1x1 Rib

(multiple of 2 sts; 1-rnd repeat)

All Rnds: *K1, p1; repeat from * to end.

NOTE

This Beret is worked from the Crown down to the Brim.

CROWN

Using dpn, CO 8 sts.

Row 1 (RS): *K1-f/b; repeat from * to end—16 sts. Divide sts among 4 needles. Join for working in the rnd, being careful not to twist sts; pm for beginning of rnd.

Rnd 2: *K1, k1-f/b; repeat from * to end—24 sts.

Rnd 3: Knit, placing marker every 3 sts (8 total markers; you may wish to use a different color marker for beginning of rnd).

Rnd 4: Purl.

Shape Crown

Note: Change to circ needle if desired to accommodate number of sts on needles (optional).

Rnd 1: *Knit, increasing 1 st (using M1 increase) randomly to marker, sm; repeat from * to end—32 sts.

Rnd 2: Knit.

Rnd 3: Repeat Rnd 1—40 sts.

Rnd 4: Purl.

Repeat Rnds 1–4, being careful to stagger M1s so that they are not always worked in the same place, until you have 26 (30) sts between markers—208 (240) sts. Work even, continuing to purl every fourth rnd, until piece measures approximately 7 (8½)" from the beginning, ending with a purl rnd.

BRIM

Shape Brim

Decrease Rnd: Decrease 42 (49) sts evenly around, using k2tog decrease—166 (191) sts remain. Knit 1 rnd.

Repeat Decrease Rnd once—124 (142) sts remain. Purl 1 rnd. Change to 1x1 Rib; work even for 4 rnds.

FINISHING

I-Cord BO

Using Backward Loop CO (see Special Techniques, page 138), CO 3 sts to left-hand needle. *K2, k2tog-tbl (third st of I-Cord together with next st from Brim), transfer sts from right-hand needle back to left-hand needle; repeat from * until all Brim sts have been worked. BO remaining I-Cord sts. Sew BO sts to Backward Loop CO.

MAKE IT YOUR OWN

If you want, you can omit the Garter ridges featured in this pattern and make a Stockinette-stitch beret instead. Or, if you want more ridges, you can work a Garter-stitch beret by alternating knit and purl rounds while randomly increasing on the knit rounds only. Remember, the rule is to increase only 8 stitches every other round, but if you skip increases on a round, you can make up for it on the next increase round. This means that if you want to incorporate a stitch pattern or a motif for a few rounds before resuming increases, you can! Just remember to keep track of your "skipped" increases and make up for them when it's more convenient.

PATTERN FEATURES
Top-down construction,
simple cables, simple shaping.

FINISHED MEASUREMENTS

21 ¼" circumference

YARN

Koigu Wool Designs Kersti Merino
Crepe (100% merino wool; 114
yards / 50 grams): 2 hanks #K1110

NEEDLES

One set of five double-pointed
needles (dpn) size US 8 (5 mm)

One 16" (40 cm) long circular (circ)
needle size US 8 (5 mm) (optional)

One 16" (40 cm) long circular needle
size US 7 (4.5 mm)

Change needle size if necessary to
obtain correct gauge.

NOTIONS

Stitch markers; cable needle (cn)

GAUGE

18 sts and 26 rows = 4" (10 cm) in
Seed stitch, using larger needles

SAND DOLLAR SLOUCH

What I like most about this cap is that the cable pattern
appears to be random when in reality it's not—it's just the
way that the Seed stitch and cables play together. This
one is worked from the top down, first working the crown
(which reminds me of a pretty sand dollar). As you get closer
to the brim, be sure to try it on to make sure you finish at
the perfect length.

ABBREVIATION

C12F: Slip 6 sts to cn, hold to front, work 6 sts in Seed st, work 6 sts in Seed st from cn.

STITCH PATTERN

Seed Stitch
(even number of sts; 1-rnd repeat)

Rnd 1: *K1, p1; repeat from * to end, end k1 if an odd number of sts.

Rnd 2: Knit the purl sts and purl the knit sts as they face you.

Repeat Rnd 2 for Seed Stitch.

NOTE

This Slouch is worked from the Crown down to the Brim.

CROWN

CO 8 sts.

Row 1: *K1-f/b; repeat from * to end—16 sts. Divide sts among 4 needles. Join for working in the rnd, being careful not to twist sts; pm for beginning of rnd.

Rnd 1: Knit.

Rnd 2: *K1, k1-f/b; repeat from * to end—24 sts.

Rnd 3: Knit, placing marker every 3 sts (8 total markers; you may wish to use a different color marker for beginning of rnd).

Shape Crown

Note: Change to circ needle if desired to accommodate number of sts on needles (optional).

Rnd 1: *K2, M1, k1, sm; repeat from * to end—32 sts.

Rnd 2: Knit.

Rnd 3: *K3, M1, k1, sm; repeat from * to end—40 sts.

Rnd 4: Knit.

Rnd 5: *K1, work in Seed st to 1 st before marker, k1, sm; repeat from * to end.

Rnd 6: *K1, work in Seed st to 1 st before marker, M1, k1, sm; repeat from * to end—48 sts.

Repeat Rnds 5 and 6, working increased sts in Seed st as they become available, until there are 14 sts between markers, ending with Rnd 6—112 sts.

Work even for 8 rnds.

Next Rnd: [K1, C12F, k1, sm, k1, work in Seed st to 1 st before marker, k1, sm] 4 times. Work even for 8 rnds.

Next Rnd: [K1, work in Seed st to 1 st before marker, k1, sm, k1, C12F, k1, sm] 4 times. Work even for 8 rnds.

Next Rnd: *K1, work 2 sts together (k2tog if second st is a knit st; p2tog if second st is a purl st), work in Seed st to 3 sts before marker, work 2 sts together, k1, sm; repeat from * to end—96 sts remain (12 sts between markers).

BRIM

Next Rnd: Change to smaller needle. [K1, p2, *k2, p2; repeat from * to 1 st before marker, k1] 8 times. Work even for 7 rnds. BO all sts in pattern.

FINISHING

Thread CO tail through CO sts. Pull tight and fasten off. Block as desired.

MAKE IT YOUR OWN

If you want more slouch, there are two easy ways to do it: You can add an extra repeat of the stitch pattern, or you can extend the ribbing at the brim. Either way, just try on as you go to make sure you like the length at each phase.

CHAPTER 3

Wrap It Up: Scarves, Shawls, Stoles, and Cowls

Many new knitters choose a basic scarf as their first knitting project. Worked flat and back and forth, scarves typically require just a couple balls of yarn and, for the most part, aren't too tricky. But when it comes to covering your neck or shoulders, there's no need to stop at scarves—there are also shawls, stoles, cowls, and shrugs, all of which offer the perfect opportunity to play with stitch patterns. And why stop at stitch patterns? Many neck-and-shoulder accessories, especially scarves, are also great for playing with shaping (i.e., they don't all have to be rectangular). Wavy, ruched, puffy, thick, thin, or coiled, neck accessories are so fun to knit, it's no wonder they remain among the most popular knitting projects of all time.

SCARVES AND SHAWLS AND WRAPS, OH MY!

Neck and shoulder accessories come in all shapes and sizes and have a variety of uses. For instance, shawls can be just about any geometric shape and are perfect for formal events; stoles tend to be rectangular and a bit shorter than shawls, just long enough to wrap around your shoulders; and scarves are typically smaller and skinnier than a shawl or stole and are worn casually. All of these "wrap" styles have been popular with knitters for centuries, and they remain popular today.

Knitting these accessories on the fly is fun because you can use just one stitch pattern or combine a number of patterns into a sampler. On the following pages are formulas for making a rectangular shawl, a circular shawl, and a triangular shawl from scratch using any yarn, dimensions, and stitch pattern. But before we dive into the formulas, let's talk about two issues that will come up in just about every scarf or shawl you'll ever make: symmetry and weaving in ends. These two issues are especially relevant since almost every type of neck accessory is flat and will be seen on both sides.

How to Make Scarves Symmetrical

Say you want to create a scarf using motifs that will look best if they travel toward the center. Rather than working it straight across (meaning that the design would be correct on one side of the scarf, but backward on the other), it's possible to show the design symmetrically. Simply cast on beginning with one edge and work half of the scarf, placing the stitches on hold when you get to the center. Then cast on the other edge and work the other half of the scarf. When you get to the center, graft the two sides together using Kitchener stitch so that the motifs both face each other and meet in the middle. This works best with stitch patterns where lacework happens on the right-side row only.

If you'd prefer not to work Kitchener stitch, you can use a provisional cast-on and work from the center of the scarf to one end, finishing with a nonrolling edge, and binding off your stitches. Then unravel the provisional cast-on, return your stitches to the needle, and work the second half in the same way you worked the first half. Your motifs will flow outward from the center of the scarf.

Another reason you might utilize a provisional cast-on is that when you knit stretchy items like stoles, or pretty much any lace project, it is imperative that your cast-on and bind-off tensions be similar. So, it makes a lot of sense to use a provisional cast-on when starting, bind off loosely with your working yarn or with a stretchy bind-off, and then go back to your provisional cast-on and try to match the same tension as your bind-off so the garment is nice and balanced after blocking.

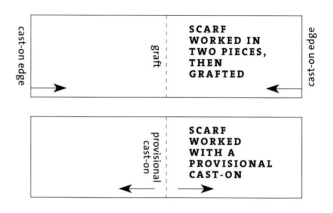

The Sparkle Ticking Wrap (page 91)
is worked lengthwise in linen stitch
with two shades of beaded silk yarn.

Spit Splicing

When it comes to hiding yarn tails, some of us are weavers and some of us are knotters. Normally, if I'm knitting a garment where the wrong side won't show, I will go ahead and weave in the ends on the wrong side of the work or maybe even (gasp) tie a knot. But when you're weaving in ends on a garment where both sides will show, such as a scarf, spit splicing is the way to go. It's a simple way to join woolen yarns and some other animal fiber blends so there is no obvious yarn end or knot showing.

Even though some knitters swear they can spit splice practically all fibers, I find that the technique doesn't work as well with cotton, linen, and hemp. With that in mind, take one end of the yarn you've been using and an end from your new ball of yarn. Loosen up the plies in each yarn end about 2 inches or so, and carefully overlap them. Now this is the "fun" part: Spit on your palm, place the overlapped yarn ends on top, and rub your two hands

together to create heat and friction. Add a little more spit if you need to (or water, but the spitting part is fun) and keep rubbing your palms together until the yarn "felts" together and becomes one continuous piece of yarn. If you plan on continuing to knit right away, try not to tug too hard on the wet part as it passes through your fingers—spit splicing creates a strong bond, but it will be a little fragile while it's still wet.

Rectangular Shawl (or Stole) Formula

Rectangular shawls, also known as stoles, are simple to design and knit because they have no shaping and can be worked widthwise or lengthwise. They're wider than scarves and are typically long enough that you can hold each end while stretching out your arms. Rectangular shawls should look good on both sides, so reversible motifs are a good choice.

1. Decide on your finished measurements (see Typical Scarf Measurements for Designing on the Fly, at left, for starting points).

2. Make a gauge swatch using your stitch pattern.

3. Carefully wash and block your gauge swatch and measure it to figure out your stitches and rows per inch (stitches per inch is most important because it affects width; you can just knit to your desired length).

4. Cast on enough stitches in the correct multiple for your motif, including extra for nonrolling edges.

5. If your motif is directional, consider casting on each end separately and working toward the center, then grafting the two ends together so that each side's motif travels inward symmetrically (see page 64 for tips on how to do this); or cast on with a provisional cast-on and work half of the piece from the center to the end, then unravel the cast-on and work the second half as for the first.

6. Work to your desired length and finish with a non-rolling border, if desired. Or, if you prefer, omit the borders and add a decorative edge either by knitting it separately and sewing it on last or knitting it and attaching it to the stole simultaneously.

TYPICAL SCARF MEASUREMENTS FOR DESIGNING ON THE FLY

There are no hard-and-fast rules for making a garment to wrap around your neck or shoulders, but there are some recommended widths and lengths. Here is a list of common measurements to get you started.

SKINNY SCARF	4 x 54"
STOLE*	16 x 70"
MUFFLER	12 x 54"
BASIC SCARF	10 x 42" or 15 x 45"

*including 6" fringe at each end

Circular Shawl Formula

Circular shawls are worked from the center out and typically start with 6 or 9 stitches joined in the round, with increases strategically placed to maintain the circular shape as the shawl grows and grows. They've enjoyed a resurgence in popularity in recent years, most likely because they are just plain fun to knit and they are a great way to use gorgeous boutique and hand-painted lace weight yarns. They are generally worn folded in half and then over the shoulders or wrapped around the neck. If you want a shawl in another shape, such as a semicircle or square, see the additional instructions on page 68.

1. Begin by casting on 6 or 9 stitches of lace weight or fingering yarn; divide them evenly among three double-pointed needles (dpns). Then join in the round and place a marker.

2. Next round, double the number of stitches using k1-f/b, M1, or yo—12 (18) stitches. Work one round even.

3. On the third round, double the number of stitches again—24 (36) stitches.

4. Work even for two rounds, and on the sixth round, double the number of stitches again—48 (72) stitches.

5. On the twelfth round, double the number of stitches again—96 (144) stitches. See a pattern emerging? As you progress through the circular shawl, you double the number of rounds you work in between increases and double the number of stitches you have on the needles every time you work an increase round.

6. Plan ahead and in non-increase sections, add motifs as you desire. If you want to fudge the number of rounds you work in between increases, or the number of stitches you increase in a round to fit a particular stitch pattern (as long as it's not a great deviation), no one will notice and your shawl will still be circular. Change to a long circular needle when your stitches no longer fit on the double-pointed needles.

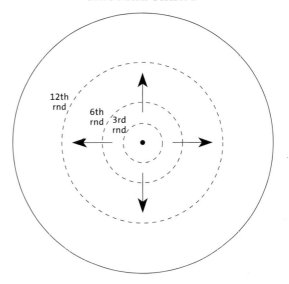

CIRCULAR SHAWL

KEY

‐ ‐ increase row/rnd

● cast-on

BEYOND THE CIRCLE

You can create a multitude of interesting shapes other than circles by starting in the center and knitting outward. All you have to do is cast on, place markers, and make evenly spaced increases at certain points to create whatever shape is in your imagination. Just like a triangular or circular shawl, inserting motifs into a square or star-shaped piece while you go can be a breeze by taking into account the number of stitches available between markers and waiting to work the stitch pattern until you have the correct multiple of stitches available. No matter which shape you choose, when the shawl is the size you like, add a few rounds of Garter stitch, or perhaps a ruffle and bind off.

Semicircle: For a semicircular shawl, follow the formula on page 67, but do not join to work in the round. Instead work the same type of increase sequence as in the formula, but in rows. For more guidance, see the Sangria Shawlette on page 83.

Square: For a square, cast on 8 stitches, double your stitch count to 16, join in the round, and place four markers (one every fourth stitch). Next round, work one increase on each side of each of the markers. You will have 32 stitches. Work one plain round. Then continue working outward, increasing on each side of every marker on every other round, adding a stitch pattern as you desire. When you bind off you will have a perfect square.

Hexagon: For a hexagon, cast on 6 or 12 stitches, double your stitch count to 12 or 24, join in the round, and place six markers (one every 2 or 4 stitches); work outward, increasing on each side of every marker every other round, adding a stitch pattern as you desire.

Octagon: For an octagon, cast on 8 stitches, double your stitch count to 16, join in the round, and place eight markers (one every 2 stitches); work outward, increasing on each side of every marker every other round, adding a stitch pattern as you desire.

SEMICIRCULAR SHAWL

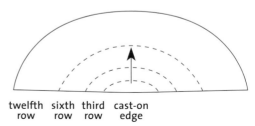

twelfth row · sixth row · third row · cast-on edge

SQUARE SHAWL

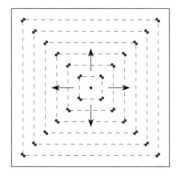

HEXAGONAL SHAWL · OCTAGONAL SHAWL

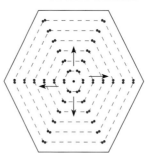
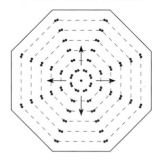

KEY

•• increase either side of marker — – increase row/rnd • cast-on

The Sangria Shawlette (page 83) is a
semicircular shawl, worked in Sangria
Lace with a Picot Point bind-off.

The Mambu Shawlette (page 74)
is a classic double triangle shawl,
worked in Bamboo Stitch.

Triangular Shawls, Two Ways: Basic and Double Triangular Shawl Formula

There are a couple different ways to make triangular shawls: A basic triangular shawl is created by working increases or decreases at the outer edges, and a double triangle shawl is created by working increases/decreases at four points (at each edge and on either side of the center stitch). Both types can be worked from the wide end, decreasing toward the point, or vice versa, which is (in my mind) the equivalent to working top down. And since I always like working top down, both of the formulas below start at the point and use increases to widen them.

Triangular shawls are a great way to show off a particular stitch pattern, yarn, or technique over a generous expanse of fabric, or they can be made just for warmth with no frills. Some triangular shawls, typically referred to as Faroese shawls, have special shaping for keeping the shawl on one's shoulders. This innovation probably came about because the folks who originated the design wore shawls while working and moving about and needed the extra help. But since I tend to wear my shawls tied in front or with a bathing suit or a tank top, I tend not to include shoulder shaping. And unless you're milking a cow or churning butter, you probably won't need shoulder shaping either.

Basic Triangle Shawl Formula

CO 3 sts.

Row 1: [K1, yo] twice, k1— 5 sts.

Row 2: Knit.

Row 3: K1, yo, knit to last st, yo, k1—7 sts.

Row 4: Knit.

Work Rows 3 and 4 until the triangle is the desired width, then bind off.

If you follow these instructions verbatim, you will make a simple Garter stitch triangle. But it's a cinch to add just about any stitch pattern—look through your stitch dictionaries and see what grabs you. You can work most of the shawl in one stitch pattern and then change to another one as you work toward the widest part of the triangle for a border or edging. As you increase the stitches, you'll notice that you might have either too

BASIC TRIANGLE

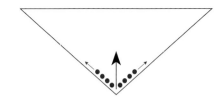

DOUBLE TRIANGLE

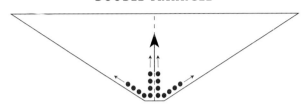

KEY

●   increase points

↑   direction of increases

many or not enough stitches to incorporate it into your motif. Don't worry. Just work those extra stitches in the background stitch (see page 27) as you normally would, knitting or purling, depending upon what would come either next or before, in pattern, and leave them there until you can complete a repeat.

Double Triangle Shawl Formula

CO 7 sts, Knit 1 row.

Row 2: [K1, yo, k2, yo] twice, k1—11 sts.

Row 3: Knit.

Row 4: [K1, yo, k4, yo] twice, k1—15 sts.

Row 5: Knit.

Continue making yo's at each end and before and after the center knit stitch on every other row until the shawl is the desired length. This will give you a Garter stitch double triangle shawl. As with the basic triangle shawl, you can spiff it up using a stitch pattern, but in this case since you are making two triangles, you'll incorporate your stitch pattern into two sections instead of one.

CHESHIRE SCARF

Garter stitch is one of those things that knitters either love or hate. I'm not the biggest fan of straight Garter-stitch anything, but when it gets broken up by rib and the pattern suddenly undulates, I kind of like it. In fact, I really do like it. This is the perfect beginner pattern—it's easy and "mindless" to create, but it produces really interesting results. And if you enjoy making this scarf so much that you're sad when it's finished, why not make the matching hat on page 39?

SCARF
Using larger needles, CO 16 sts.

Section One

Begin Garter st; work even for 22 rows (11 ridges). Change to smaller needles.

Section Two

Row 1: K7, p2, k7.

Row 2: K3, p4, k2, p4, k3.

Rows 3-12: Repeat Rows 1 and 2.

Change to larger needles.

Repeat Sections One and Two until piece measures approximately 80" from the beginning, ending with a completed Section One. BO all sts knitwise.

FINISHING
Block as desired.

MAKE IT YOUR OWN

If you want a scarf with a more random pattern, experiment with varying the length of the Garter sections or rib sections. Or, experiment with a scarf that is entirely made of rib, but use two drastically different needle sizes, switching from one to the other every few inches or so.

FINISHED MEASUREMENTS

5 ¼" wide (measured across Section One) x 80" long

YARN

Berroco Peruvia Quick (100% Peruvian highland wool; 103 yards / 100 grams): 2 hanks #9127 Palomino Blue

NEEDLES

One pair straight needles size US 11 (8 mm)

One pair straight needles size US 9 (5.5 mm)

Change needle size if necessary to obtain correct gauge.

GAUGE

12 sts and 22 rows = 4" (10 cm) in Garter stitch, using larger needles

15 sts and 20 rows = 4" (10 cm) in st pattern from Section Two, using smaller needles

PATTERN FEATURES
Simple stitch pattern,
simple shaping.

FINISHED MEASUREMENTS

20" long from CO edge to BO edge, measured along center st

Approximately 80" at BO edge (see schematic)

YARN

Misti Alpaca Hand Paint Baby Suri Silk (80% baby suri alpaca / 20% silk; 218 yards / 100 grams): 2 hanks #SP19 Golden Cradle

NEEDLES

One 29" (70 cm) long or longer circular (circ) needle size US 5 (3.75 mm)

Change needle size if necessary to obtain correct gauge.

NOTIONS

Removable stitch marker

GAUGE

16 sts and 22 rows = 4" (10 cm) in Bamboo Stitch

MAMBU SHAWLETTE

I love little shawls. You can throw them on or tie them any old way and they always work out as a chic accessory. Shoot, I even like tying these little shawls onto my purse handle for a bit of punch. (My sister-in-law used to do that with her Hermès scarves, so I thought, "Why not knit ones, too?") Even though the stitch pattern I chose here looks tricky, it's actually very simple to execute. Shaping is a snap, too, because increases are only made along the edges and the center sections (which means you don't have to worry about working a stitch pattern while increasing).

STITCH PATTERN

Bamboo Stitch

(multiple of 2 sts; 2-row repeat)

Row 1 (RS): K1, *yo, k2, pass yo over k2; repeat from * to last st, k1.

Row 2: Purl.

Repeat Rows 1 and 2 for Bamboo Stitch.

SHAWLETTE

CO 11 sts.

Shape Shawlette

Row 1 (RS): K1, yo, k4, yo, k1 (pm on st to mark center; move marker up every few rows), yo, k4, yo, k1—15 sts.

Row 2: K1, yo, p6, yo, p1 (center st), yo, p6, yo, k1—19 sts.

Row 3: K1, yo, k1, *yo, k2, pass yo over k2; repeat from * to 1 st before marked center st, [k1, yo] twice, k1, *yo, k2, pass yo over k2; repeat from * to last 2 sts, k1, yo, k1—23 sts.

Row 4: K1, yo, purl to marked center st, yo, p1 (center st), yo, purl to last st, yo, k1—27 sts.

Repeat Rows 3 and 4, increasing 4 sts every row, and working increased sts in Bamboo Stitch, until you have 291 sts.

Next Row (RS): *K1-f/b; repeat from * to end—582 sts. Work even in St st for 5 rows, beginning with a purl row. BO all sts.

FINISHING

Block lightly.

MAKE IT YOUR OWN

Use a solid color yarn to emphasize the stitch pattern—a nice, natural color like tan or a heathered earth tone would be lovely. Since gauge isn't an issue, you could also cast on using a bulkier yarn for a more substantial wrap.

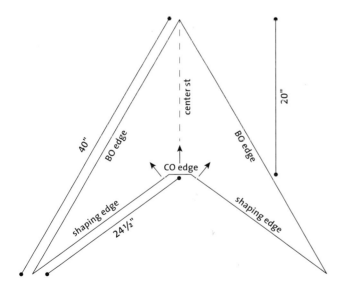

40"

center st

20"

BO edge

BO edge

CO edge

shaping edge

shaping edge

24½"

PATTERN FEATURES
Ribbing, stranded (Fair Isle)
colorwork, no shaping.

FINISHED MEASUREMENTS
23 ¾" circumference x 7 ¼" tall

YARN
**Misti Alpaca Worsted (100% baby
alpaca; 109 yards / 50 grams):
1 skein each #3780 Raspberry Sorbet
(MC) and #5470 Pottery Melange (A)**

NEEDLES
**One 20" (50 cm) long circular (circ)
needle size US 7 (4.5 mm)**

**Change needle size if necessary to
obtain correct gauge.**

NOTIONS
Stitch marker

GAUGE
**20 sts and 22 rows = 4" (10 cm) in
Fair Isle Pattern from Chart**

PRETZEL HEART COWL

I like to think of a cowl as a scarf that won't fall off.
If you're looking for a quick knit to give to a friend—or to
yourself for that matter—Pretzel Heart Cowl is a good
choice. The colorwork portions are super easy since you'll
only wrangle two colors at a time and the color changes
aren't very frequent.

STITCH PATTERN

1x1 Rib

(multiple of 2 sts; 1-rnd repeat)

All Rnds: *K1, p1; repeat from * to end.

COWL

CO 118 sts. Join for working in the rnd, being careful not to twist sts; pm for beginning of rnd. Begin 1x1 Rib; work even for 5 rnds, increase 1 st at beginning of last rnd—119 sts.

Next Rnd: Change to Fair Isle Pattern from Chart; work even until 2 vertical repeats of Chart have been completed.

Next Rnd: Change to 1x1 Rib; work even for 5 rnds, decrease 1 st at beginning of first rnd—118 sts remain. BO all sts in pattern.

FINISHING

Block as desired.

FAIR ISLE PATTERN

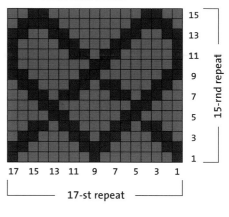

15-rnd repeat

17-st repeat

KEY

Knit all sts. ■ MC ■ A

MAKE IT YOUR OWN

If you're not in the mood for colorwork, simply skip it and use a self-patterning yarn instead. Or for extra fun, use scraps of yarn in the same weight and make stripes. Since many cowls (including this one) are typically the same circumference as caps, you can easily transform this pattern into a hat. Cast on and work ribbing for a couple inches, change to Stockinette stitch (include the colorwork, or not) for approximately 6 inches, and shape the top as you would a cap. In this case, you will have 118 stitches on your needles when it is time to shape the top of the cap. To set up the crown, decrease 4 stitches evenly (114 stitches will remain). Then separate the cap into six sections using five markers, with 19 stitches in each section. On the next round and every third round, decrease 12 stitches as follows: *K2tog, work to 2 stitches before the next marker, ssk; repeat from the * to the end. When there are 6 stitches left, cut yarn, leaving a long tail, and thread it through the live stitches. Cinch tight and weave in the end on the wrong side of your new cap.

SANGRIA SHAWLETTE

This is the perfect little shawl to add a punch of color to your day (or night). The semicircular construction keeps things interesting and the lace portion is just a 6-stitch/6-row repeat, making it super easy to memorize. I have to confess: I don't typically design or knit a lot of lace, but now I find myself wondering if I'll make this shawlette again in a different fiber . . . linen, perhaps? Or maybe hemp?

STITCH PATTERNS

Sangria Lace
Note: You may work pattern from text or Chart.
(multiple of 6 sts; 6-row repeat)

Row 1 (RS): *K1, ssk, yo, k1, yo, k2tog; repeat from * to end.

Rows 2 and 4: Purl.

Row 3: *K1, yo, sk2p, yo, k2tog, yo; repeat from * to end.

Row 5: *K2, yo, sk2p, yo, k1; repeat from * to end.

Row 6: Repeat Row 2.

Repeat Rows 1–6 for Sangria Lace.

Picot Point BO
(multiple of 3 sts + 2)

BO 2 sts, *slip st back to left-hand needle, CO 2 sts, BO 4 sts; repeat from * to end.

NOTE

This semicircular Shawlette is worked from the center upper cast-on edge outwards. It will take almost all of the yardage in the yarn specified, so if your gauge isn't correct or if you plan on making it larger, be sure to buy extra yarn.

FINISHED MEASUREMENTS
78 ½" wide along BO edge
18 ½" long at center

YARN
Twisted Sisters Zazu (100% extrafine merino wool; 390 yards / 50 grams): 1 hank Thai Chili

NEEDLES
One 29" (70 cm) long or longer circular (circ) needle size US 5 (3.75 mm)

Change needle size if necessary to obtain correct gauge.

NOTIONS
Stitch markers

GAUGE
20 sts and 28 rows = 4" (10 cm) in Stockinette stitch (St st)

SHAWL

CO 3 sts. Knit 6 rows; do not turn after final row. Rotate piece to the right, pick up and knit 3 sts along side edge; rotate piece to the right, pick up and knit 3 sts along CO edge—9 sts.

Row 1 (WS): K3, pm, p3, pm, k3.

Row 2: K3, sm, *k1, yo; repeat from * to marker, sm, k3—12 sts.

Rows 3-5: Work even, keeping first and last 3 sts in Garter st, and sts between markers in St st.

Row 6: Repeat Row 2—18 sts.

Rows 7-11: Repeat Row 3.

Row 12: Repeat Row 2—30 sts.

Rows 13-23: Repeat Row 3.

Row 24: Repeat Row 2—54 sts.

Row 25: Repeat Row 3.

Rows 26-37: Keeping first and last 3 sts in Garter st, and working sts between markers in Sangria Lace, work 2 vertical repeats of Sangria Lace.

Rows 38 and 39: Repeat Row 3.

Row 40: Repeat Row 2—102 sts.

Rows 41-51: Repeat Row 3.

Rows 52-69: Keeping first and last 3 sts in Garter st, and working sts between markers in Sangria Lace, work 3 vertical repeats of Sangria Lace.

Rows 70 and 71: Repeat Row 3.

Row 72: Repeat Row 2—198 sts.

Rows 73-83: Repeat Row 3.

Rows 84-113: Keeping first and last 3 sts in Garter st, and working sts between markers in Sangria Lace, work 5 vertical repeats of Sangria Lace.

Rows 114 and 115: Repeat Row 3.

Row 116: Repeat Row 2—390 sts.

Rows 117-123: Repeat Row 3.

Row 124: Knit, increasing 2 sts evenly—392 sts.

Row 125: Repeat Row 5.

BO all sts using Picot Point BO.

FINISHING

Block as desired.

MAKE IT YOUR OWN

For a striped version of this shawl, you could use a contrasting yarn color for the Stockinette portions. You could even substitute the fiber, using linen or maybe bamboo, for a decidedly different "look." Instead of the Picot Point bind-off, try creating a ruffle by working one wrong-side row of the Stockinette portion toward the end, and then, on the next row, increasing your stitch count by knitting one stitch and then knitting into the front and back on the next stitch. (You'll have tons of stitches on the needles but the effect will be glorious). Then, work an inch or so of Stockinette, a few rows of Garter (knit every row), and then bind off. (And if you do this, please send me a picture!)

SANGRIA LACE

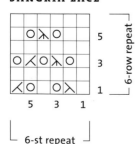

5

3

1

6-row repeat

6-st repeat

KEY

☐ Knit on RS, purl on WS.

○ Yo

╱ K2tog

╲ Ssk

人 Sk2p

PATTERN FEATURES
Provisional cast-on,
lace pattern, no shaping.

FINISHED MEASUREMENTS

15 ½" wide x 53" long, before blocking

14 ¼" wide x 65 ½" long, after blocking

YARN

The Sanguine Gryphon Gala Fingering (60% silk / 40% cashmere; 210 yards / 2 ounces): 2 hanks Cornflower

NEEDLES

One pair straight needles size US 4 (3.5 mm)

Change needle size if necessary to obtain correct gauge.

NOTIONS

Waste yarn; stitch markers (optional)

GAUGE

21 sts and 32 rows = 4" (10 cm) in Chevron and Eyelet patterns, before blocking

23 sts and 22 rows = 4" (10 cm) in Chevron and Eyelet patterns, after blocking

SKYLARK STOLE

This stole turned me into a lace lover. In the old days I wondered why anyone would ever want to knit something with so many intentional holes in it and that requires such concentration. But someone smart gave me an idea: Separate the motifs using markers, so if you miss a yarnover or get confused, you only have to troubleshoot within that one group of stitches. I must say, this tip changed my outlook on the whole lace-knitting enterprise. I combined two motifs for this stole to make winglike shapes, but if you look closely, they're actually Ws, which, I admit, was a sweet surprise.

STITCH PATTERNS

Eyelet Pattern

Note: You may work pattern from text or Chart.

(panel of 4 sts; 2-row repeat)

Row 1 and all WS Rows: Purl.

Row 2: Yo, ssk, k2tog, yo.

Repeat Rows 1 and 2 for Eyelet Pattern.

Chevron Pattern

Note: You may work pattern from text or Chart.

(panel of 21 sts; 14-row repeat)

Row 1 and all WS Rows: Purl.

Row 2: K1, [yo, ssk, k2tog, yo, k1] 4 times.

Row 4: K2, yo, ssk, k3, k2tog, yo, k3, yo, ssk, k3, k2tog, yo, k2.

Row 6: K3, yo, ssk, k1, k2tog, yo, k5, yo, ssk, k1, k2tog, yo, k3.

Row 8: K4, yo, sk2p, yo, k7, yo, sk2p, yo, k4.

Rows 10, 12, and 14: K1, [ssk, k2, yo, k1, yo, k2, k2tog, k1] twice.

Repeat Rows 1–14 for Chevron Pattern.

NOTE

To make the Eyelet and Chevron patterns easier to work, you may wish to place markers between patterns.

STOLE

Using waste yarn and Provisional CO, CO 83 sts. Knit 2 rows.

Next Row (WS): K2 (edge sts; keep in Garter st [knit every row]), [work 4 sts in Eyelet Pattern, then 21 sts in Chevron Pattern] 3 times, work 4 sts in Eyelet Pattern, k2 (edge sts; keep in Garter st).

Work even until piece measures approximately 53" from the beginning, ending with Row 1 of Eyelet Pattern. Knit 2 rows. BO all sts loosely.

FINISHING

Carefully unravel Provisional CO and place sts on needle. BO all sts loosely. Block to measurements.

EYELET PATTERN

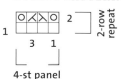

KEY

☐	Knit on RS, purl on WS.
ⓞ	Yo
⟋	K2tog
⟍	Ssk
⅄	Sk2p

CHEVRON PATTERN

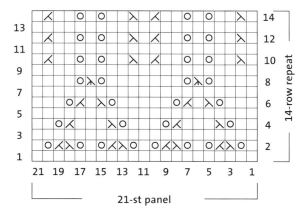

21-st panel

MAKE IT YOUR OWN

Since gauge isn't really an issue here, it's easy to try out different yarn weights. Make a gauge swatch with one full repeat of the motif (4 stitches in Eyelet Pattern followed by 21 stitches in Chevron Pattern), then wash and block. If you like what you see, measure the motif, decide how wide you want your stole to be, and use this measurement to decide how many repeats of the motif will fit within the width, including the final repeat of the Eyelet Pattern and border on either side. Of course, you need to be sure you have enough yarn (see page 17 for tips on estimating yardage).

The variation of the Skylark Stole shown at right uses a heavier yarn, but I wanted the stole to be the same basic size as the original. To do this, I swatched an entire repeat of the motif, washed and blocked it, then determined how many stitches I could cast on to end up with a stole of a similar size. The swatch read 3 stitches per inch compared to 5.25 in the original. That said, I decided that I would keep the first and last 4 stitches in Garter stitch and rearrange the lace a little bit as follows: 4 stitches of Eyelet Pattern, followed by 21 stitches of Chevron Pattern, followed by another 4 stitches of the Eyelet Pattern. This variation was worked with three hanks of The Sanguine Gryphon Codex in Hannah Quick.

PATTERN FEATURES
Simple stitch pattern,
no shaping, fringe.

SPARKLE TICKING WRAP

To me, this sparkly beaded-and-sequined wrap looks a little bit like a glorious version of pillow ticking. The yarn is prebeaded, but if you want to add beads to yarn you already have on hand, take a look at page 139 and add the beads as you knit.

STITCH PATTERNS

Linen Stitch
(odd number of sts; 2-row repeat)

Row 1 (RS): K1, *slip 1 wyif, k1; repeat from * to end.

Row 2: P2, *slip 1 wyib, p1; repeat from * to last st, p1.

Repeat Rows 1 and 2 for Linen Stitch.

Stripe Pattern
Working in Linen Stitch, *work 2 rows each in A, B, C, D, C, then B; repeat from * for Stripe Pattern.

WRAP

Using A, CO 205 sts. Begin Stripe Pattern; work even until 7 vertical repeats of Stripe Pattern have been completed. Change to A; work even for 2 rows. BO all sts.

FINISHING

Cut approximately sixty 10" strands of C. Using crochet hook and single strand for each Fringe, work Fringe (see Special Techniques, page 138) along both short ends. Trim ends.

MAKE IT YOUR OWN

Since this wrap is worked lengthwise, you can easily make it into a skinny scarf; just stop knitting when it has reached the desired width, maybe 4 inches or so. Or, you could make it wider for a more substantial wrap. Another option is to make it into a masculine scarf by omitting the beads and sequins and using a different fiber, like wool or a wool blend.

FINISHED MEASUREMENTS

51 ¼" wide x 8 ¾" long, not including Fringe

YARN

Tilli Tomas Plie (100% plied silk; 125 yards / 50 grams): 1 hank each Rattan (A) and Parchment (B)

Tilli Tomas Disco Lights (90% spun silk / 10% petite sequins; 225 yards / 100 grams): 1 hank Parchment (C)

Tilli Tomas Beaded Plie (100% silk with glass beads; 120 yards / 50 grams): 1 hank Glazed Ginger (D)

NEEDLES

One 32" (80 cm) long or longer circular (circ) needle size US 8 (5 mm)

Change needle size if necessary to obtain correct gauge.

NOTIONS

Crochet hook size US H/8 (5 mm), for Fringe

GAUGE

16 sts and 40 rows = 4" (10 cm) in Linen Stitch

FINISHED MEASUREMENTS

7" wide x 73" long, not including
Fringe

YARN

Blue Sky Alpacas Bulky (50% alpaca /
50% wool; 45 yards / 100 grams):
5 hanks #1217 Curry

NEEDLES

One pair straight needles size US 15
(10 mm)

NOTIONS

Crochet hook size US N/15 (10 mm)
for Fringe (optional)

GAUGE

10 sts and 10 rows = 4" (10 cm) in
Smocking Pattern

*Note: Gauge isn't essential for this
project. However, having a different
st gauge will affect the width of the
Scarf, and might affect the amount
of yarn required.*

SMOCKED

I'm one of those knitters who gets a little annoyed when both sides of a garment will be seen, but the wrong side doesn't look good. So, I like to make sure that nearly everything I design has a decent-looking backside (insert another joke here). This bulky scarf looks good on both sides, and despite its length, it's a fast knit. The "wraps" in the stitch pattern are especially fun to do—once you knit this scarf, I bet you'll be itching to use the technique again and again. In fact, it's so much fun that I'm surprised there aren't more stitch patterns out there using this effect.

STITCH PATTERN

Smocking Pattern

(multiple of 8 sts + 10; 8-row repeat)

Row 1 (WS): K2, *p2, k2; repeat from * to end.

Rows 2 and 3: Knit the knit sts and purl the purl sts as they face you.

Row 4: P2, *yb, insert right-hand needle from the front in between sixth and seventh sts on left-hand needle, draw up a loop and place it on left-hand needle, k2tog (loop together with next st on left-hand needle), k1, p2, k2, p2; repeat from * to end.

Rows 5-7: Repeat Row 2.

Row 8: P2, k2, p2, *yb, insert right-hand needle from the front in between sixth and seventh sts on left-hand needle, draw up a loop and place it on left-hand needle, k2tog (loop together with next st on left-hand needle), k1, p2, k2, p2; repeat from * to last 4 sts, k2, p2.

Repeat Rows 1–8 for Smocking Pattern.

NOTE

If you prefer a wider Scarf, add sts in multiples of 8. Remember, if you widen the Scarf, you may require additional yarn.

SCARF

CO 18 sts. Knit 2 rows. Begin Smocking Pattern; work even until piece measures approximately 72" from the beginning, ending with Row 3 of Smocking Pattern. Knit 2 rows. BO all sts knitwise.

FINISHING

Fringe (optional)

Cut forty 10" strands of yarn. Using 2 strands of yarn held together, work 10 Fringes (see Special Techniques, page 138) along each short end of Scarf.

MAKE IT YOUR OWN

It's a cinch to turn this scarf into the cowl shown here. In the variation, I cast on 26 stitches provisionally and worked the stitch pattern for about 22 inches, ending on Row 2 of the stitch pattern. After that, I put the provisional stitches on an extra needle, placed the right sides together, and did a three-needle bind off (see Special Techniques, page 138). This variation was worked with two hanks of Blue Sky Alpacas Bulky in #1003 Porcupine.

TIPSY PASHMINA

Here's a scarf that looks great on both sides with little fanfare except for the tiny pom-poms that line each edge. The stitch pattern looks tilted but is actually worked straight—the small areas of bias lace mesh pull the blocks diagonally, forming the unusual pattern.

FINISHED MEASUREMENTS

Approximately 50" long x 6" wide

YARN

Madelinetosh Pashmina (75% superwash merino wool / 15% silk / 10% cashmere; 360 yards / 100 grams): 1 hank Filigree

NEEDLES

One pair straight needles size US 4 (3.5 mm)

Change needle size if necessary to obtain correct gauge.

NOTIONS

¾" pom-pom maker

GAUGE

22 sts and 30 rows = 4" in Tilting Blocks

STITCH PATTERN

Tilting Blocks
(multiple of 16 sts + 1; 16-row repeat)

Rows 1, 3, 5, and 7 (RS): *[Ssk, yo] 4 times, k8; repeat from * to last st, k1.

Rows 2, 4, 6, and 8: *K9, p7; repeat from * to last st, k1.

Rows 9, 11, 13, and 15: K1, *k8, [yo, k2tog] 4 times; repeat from * to end.

Rows 10, 12, 14, and 16: P1, *p7, k9; repeat from * to end.

Repeat Rows 1–16 for Tilting Blocks.

SCARF

CO 33 sts. Begin Tilting Blocks; work even until piece measures approximately 50" from the beginning, ending with Row 7 or 15 of pattern. BO all sts in pattern, working Row 8 or 16 as you BO.

FINISHING

Block lightly. Using pom-pom maker, make 6 pom-poms and attach them to each of the three points at each end of the Scarf.

MAKE IT YOUR OWN

You can make a stole using this pattern by adding multiple repeats of the stitch pattern, or you can subtract a repeat and turn it into a skinny head wrap. Pom-poms are fun for some but aren't for everyone. If you fall into the "non-pom-pom" category, you can leave them off and use a fringe instead; or use no edging and leave the edges plain. You are in charge, after all.

PATTERN FEATURES

Top-down construction, simple shaping, stranded (Fair Isle) colorwork.

SKIPPER PONCHO

So what if ponchos come and go in the fashion world? As long as they aren't sporting hippie fringe and they don't squeeze you like a sausage, I think they are versatile, dramatic, and jaunty all at the same time. Throw this one on over your swimsuit or wear it with a tank and jeans. I worked it from the top down and in the round, adding shaping to soften the "points" you usually get in the front and back of a typical poncho.

PONCHO

With longer circ needle and MC, CO 56 (64, 72) sts. Begin St st, beginning with a knit row, place marker every 7 (8, 9) sts (7 markers placed). Purl 1 row.

Shape Yoke

Increase Row (RS): Continuing in St st, increase 1 st randomly in each section (8 increases per row) this row, then every other row 20 (23, 26) times, making sure

SIZES

Small (Medium, Large)

FINISHED MEASUREMENTS

40 ¾ (46 ½, 52 ¼)" circumference, at shoulders

53 (60 ¼, 66 ¼)" circumference, at lower edge

YARN

Lorna's Laces Honor (70% baby alpaca / 30% silk; 275 yards / 100 grams): 2 (3, 3) hanks Blackberry (MC); 1 hank Turquoise (A)

NEEDLES

One 36" (90 cm) long or longer circular (circ) needle size US 6 (4 mm)

One 24" (60 cm) long circular needle size US 6 (4 mm)

Change needle size if necessary to obtain correct gauge.

NOTIONS

Stitch markers; 4 or more ¾" beads

GAUGE

22 sts and 24 rows = 4" (10 cm) in Stockinette stitch (St st)

not to stack increases on top of each other—224 (256, 288) sts [28 (32, 36) sts each section]. Purl 1 row, removing all markers.

Joining Row (RS): K112 (128, 144), pm, knit to end. Join for working in the rnd; pm for beginning of rnd. Knit 2 rnds.

Shape Body

Increase Rnd: Increase 4 sts this rnd, every other rnd 4 times, then every 6 rnds 8 (10, 10) times, as follows: [K1-f/b, knit to 1 st before marker, k1-f/b, sm] twice—276 (316, 348) sts.

Next Rnd: Work across sts from Chart A; work even until entire Chart is complete. Working in MC only, repeat Increase Rnd once—280 (320, 352) sts.

Next Rnd: Work across sts from Chart B; work even until entire Chart is complete. Continuing in A only, repeat Increase Rnd this rnd, then every 6 rnds twice—292 (332, 364) sts. Knit to second marker; this is new beginning of rnd marker. Purl 1 rnd. Knit 1 rnd. Purl 1 rnd. BO all sts knitwise.

FINISHING

Neckband

With RS facing, using shorter circ needle and MC, pick up and knit 1 st for every st along CO edge, pm, and approximately 2 sts for every 3 rows along Left and Right Fronts. Join for working in the rnd; pm for beginning of rnd.

Next Rnd: *K2, yo; repeat from * to marker, sm, knit to end.

Next Rnd: Knit to marker. BO all sts knitwise.

Cord Tie

Cut one 72"-long strand each of MC and A. Holding strands together, fold in half and secure one end to a stationary object. Twist from other end until the cord begins to buckle. Fold twisted length in half and holding ends together, allow to twist up on itself. Slide half of beads onto cut end and tie end in an overhand knot to secure. Thread opposite end through eyelets in top of Neckband; thread remaining beads onto this end, and tie to secure. Trim ends.

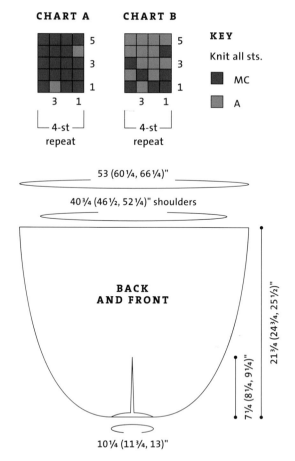

CHART A   CHART B   KEY

Knit all sts.

■ MC
■ A

4-st repeat   4-st repeat

53 (60¼, 66¼)"

40¾ (46½, 52¼)" shoulders

BACK AND FRONT

21¾ (24¾, 25½)"

7¼ (8¼, 9¼)"

10¼ (11¾, 13)"

Note: Piece is worked from the top down.

MAKE IT YOUR OWN

If you want, you can shorten the neck opening by trying it on as you go and joining the poncho in the round earlier than the pattern directs. Swap out the color changes for stripes or insert a Fair Isle motif from a stitch dictionary (just make sure you have the right multiple of stitches to accommodate the pattern multiple). Or keep it simple and omit all color changes for a classic one-color poncho.

CHAPTER 4

Perfect Pairs:
Gloves, Mitts, Socks,
and Leg Warmers

Ah, mittens and socks . . . the perfect, portable, knitted accessories! So much fun you can't knit just one! (Har har, had to throw that in.) In this chapter, I've grouped together the accessories that keep our hands and feet warm (and sometimes our arms and legs, too), all of which are customizable, quick, and happen to come in pairs.

HANDS AND ARMS

Accessories for hands and arms go by many names. Gloves have separate coverings for each finger and thumb; if they have openings but no covering for the fingers, they're called fingerless gloves. Gloves that cover the entire hand but do not have separate finger openings are called mittens. And then there are arm warmers, which are probably modeled after leg warmers, but (you guessed it) are worn on your arms. No matter what type of hand or arm accessory you want to knit, this chapter has you covered. I like to make mine simple and fun, but if you want to spice things up, use the formula on page 106 and add a stitch pattern of your choice.

HAND MEASUREMENTS

To work perfectly fitted mittens or gloves, all you need to know is the circumference of your hand or the circumference of the intended wearer's hand. Use a flexible tape measure and measure the circumference at the knuckles or widest part of the hand above the thumb.

If the person you're making the mittens or gloves for isn't available for measurements (maybe it's a surprise gift?), you can use the chart below and estimate the size.

Circumference of Hand

2-4 YEARS	4-6 YEARS	6-8 YEARS	8 YEARS/ WOMEN'S SMALL	WOMEN'S MEDIUM	WOMEN'S LARGE/ MEN'S SMALL	MEN'S MEDIUM	MEN'S LARGE
5 ½"	6"	6 ½"	7"	7 ½"	8"	8 ½"	9"

The Dartmoor Mittens (page 122) are classic mittens with a fun stitch pattern worked up the backside.

Simple Fingerless Mitts Formula

I love to whip up fingerless mitts with a skein of sock yarn, but if you follow this formula you can use any yarn in any gauge you like. If you want to make these mitts a little less super simple, read the next section on thumb gussets and "afterthought" thumbs, then add one on the fly.

1. Do a gauge swatch.

2. Take your hand measurement.

3. Using needles one size smaller than the ones you used for your gauge swatch, cast on enough stitches to equal your hand measurement, rounding to an even number for 1x1 rib, or to a number divisible by 4 for 2x2 rib.

4. Join in the round and work in ribbing for about 1½ inches, or to desired ribbing length.

5. Change to larger needles and work in Stockinette stitch until the mitten reaches just above your thumb joint.

6. Bind off 8 stitches at the beginning of the next round (or about an inch worth of stitches).

7. At the end of that round, cast on 8 stitches just above those that you bound off.

8. Work in Stockinette stitch again until the mitten is just over your knuckles.

9. Change to ribbing again, for about an inch. Bind off.

WANT TO TRANSFORM YOUR FINGERLESS MITTS INTO MITTENS?

If you have a fingerless mitten pattern on your hands, but you want to make traditional mittens with a closed top, never fear—you won't have to troll the Internet to find another mitten pattern to follow. First, work the body of the fingerless mitts, but continue knitting until it reaches to the base of your middle fingernail. Next round, reduce the number of stitches so that they are divisible by 6 or 8, and on the next round, place 6 or 8 markers evenly around. Work one decrease round by decreasing after each marker, then work one plain round. Continue decreasing in this manner until you have 6 or 8 stitches left. Cut the yarn, thread it through the remaining stitches, and fasten off. Then, work the thumb as in the pattern but stop when it reaches the base of your thumbnail. Last, work your thumb decreases as for the body of the mitten, making decrease rounds every other round until you have 6 or 8 stitches on the needles. Cut the yarn and thread it through the live stitches, then fasten off.

Thumb Openings Three Ways

Glove patterns will almost always include instructions for gussets, but mitten and fingerless-mitten patterns don't always have them. Mittens and fingerless mittens are simple tubes, so a slit or a hole are usually the easiest ways to deal with making room for your thumb. Plus, they can be added at the last minute, when you've reached the base of the thumb, while gussets require a little more forethought.

Thumb gussets are triangular-shaped areas of extra knitted fabric that give additional room at points of stress and allow you to move your thumb more freely. These gussets are worked at the same time as the rest of the piece and are set off by a couple of markers that are placed at the halfway mark through the entire circumference of the glove or mitten, after you have completed the wrist ribbing. Although it is totally fine to use a slit (like the Canoodle Arm Warmers on page 127) or a hole (like the Daffodil Mitts on page 119), some knitters insist that thumb gussets are absolutely necessary and will pooh-pooh any pattern that doesn't have them.

The good news is, even if you want to knit a mitten pattern that doesn't have thumb gussets, you can add them without a second thought. Just know that you'll need several extra yards of yarn per glove or mitten and that if the mitten or glove has a stitch pattern that flows all the way around, you may have to consider a gusset that has a plain background or do some math to incorporate the stitch pattern within the gusset. So, let's talk about the thumb gusset first and then I'll show you how to do a simple "afterthought" thumb opening and a simple slit opening for fingerless mitts.

THUMB GUSSET FORMULA

1. Keeping things simple, place stitches on four double-pointed needles (dpns) or two circular (circ) needles: One-half of the stitches on the first two dpns (or one circ) and the other half of the stitches on the last two dpns (or other circ). For the right hand, the first two dpns (or first circ) hold the back-of-the-hand stitches, and vice versa for the left hand.

2. Once the wrist stitches have been completed and the mitten reaches the base of the thumb, work to the end of the second dpn, or to the end of the needle that holds the stitches for the back of the hand, place a marker, increase 1 stitch to create a center gusset stitch, place a marker, work to the end of the round. You will have one gusset stitch between the markers.

3. Work one round even.

4. Increase Round 1: Work to the first marker, slip the marker, increase 1 stitch, k1, increase 1 stitch, slip the marker, and work to the end—2 stitches increased and 3 gusset stitches between the markers.

5. Work two rounds even.

6. Increase Round 2: Work to the first marker, slip the marker, increase 1 stitch, work to the second marker, increase 1 stitch, slip the marker, and work to the end—2 stitches increased and 5 gusset stitches between the markers.

7. Continue working increase rounds on every third round as established until the gusset measures about 3 inches wide for an adult (for example, you'll have about 15 stitches with a gauge of 5 stitches per inch). If the height of the gusset doesn't reach the place on your hand where the thumb separates from your palm, work an extra few rounds without increasing. (Typical gusset heights are between 2 and 2 ½ inches for an adult.)

8. On the next round, work to the marker separating the gusset stitches, transfer the gusset stitches onto waste yarn, removing the markers, and work to the end. Continue working your mitten or glove as written in your pattern.

9. Now it is time to work your thumb stitches: Transfer the held stitches evenly to three dpns. Join yarn at the right-hand edge of the stitches and work across the gusset stitches, pick up a few stitches to close the hole, and join to work in the round. For a topless thumb, work a few rounds and change to a nonrolling edging before binding off. For a closed thumb, work even until the thumb tube just reaches the end of the thumb.

10. Decrease Round: *K2tog; repeat from * to the end, working a k3tog at the end if you had an odd number of stitches on the needles. Break the yarn and draw the tail through the remaining stitches and fasten off.

The fingerless Dartmoor Mittens
(page 125) have a gusset and
a topless thumb.

"AFTERTHOUGHT" THUMB FORMULA

If you don't want to bother with a gusset, you can make an "afterthought" thumb by picking up live stitches after the mitt is complete, working the thumb in the round, then binding off. Just grab some brightly colored waste yarn in the same gauge and start working your mitten. (For an example, see the Daffodil Mitts below.)

1. Place the stitches on four double-pointed needles (dpns) or two circular (circ) needles: One-half of the stitches on the first two dpns (or one circ) and the other half of the stitches on the last two dpns (or other circ). For the right hand, the first two dpns (or first circ) hold the back-of-the-hand stitches, and vice versa for the left hand.

2. Once the wrist stitches have been completed and the mitten reaches the base of the thumb, work to the end of the second dpn, or to the end of the needle that holds the stitches for the back of the hand, break the working yarn, and work approximately 1½ inches worth of stitches with the waste yarn. Alternatively, you could skip breaking the yarn and, instead, work the stitches in your brightly colored waste yarn, slip them back onto the left needle, and then work across them again in the working yarn—two fewer ends to weave in!

3. Break the waste yarn and join the working yarn. Complete the mitten as instructed.

4. Carefully pick out the waste yarn to expose the thumb stitches and place the bottom and top live stitches onto three dpns.

5. Join the yarn and work across the first needle, pick up and knit 1 or 2 stitches from the gap between the top and the bottom stitches, and continue across the needle, holding the top stitches, and when you get to the second gap, pick up and knit 1 or 2 stitches.

6. Place a marker and join to work in the round. For a topless thumb, work a few rounds and change to a non-rolling edging before binding off.

7. For a closed thumb, work even until the thumb tube just reaches the end of the thumb.

8. Decrease Round: *K2tog; repeat from * to the end, working k3tog at the end if you had an odd number of stitches on the needles. Break the yarn and draw the tail through the remaining stitches and fasten off.

SPLIT-STYLE SIMPLE THUMB OPENING

A split-style thumb opening is simply a slit created by switching from working in the round to working flat. To create this basic thumb opening for fingerless mitts, work half the stitches (back-of-hand stitches) and place a marker. When you have reached the place in your knitting where the base of your thumb is, begin working back and forth instead of in the round and work the first and last few stitches in a nonrolling edging, such as Garter stitch or Seed stitch. Continue working the mitten flat for approximately 2½ inches, or the desired height of your thumb opening, and then resume working in the round again (discontinuing the edging stitches) until you want to bind off. Take a look at the Canoodle Arm Warmers on page 127 for an example of how it is done.

The Daffodil Mitts (page 119) have an "afterthought" topless thumb opening.

FEET AND LEGS

Many knitters feel great passion for accessories that go on your feet and legs. (Seriously, there are sock knitters that travel across the country or overseas just to meet other sock knitters; they have their socks with them on needles wherever they go. When it comes to enthusiasm, the sock knitters get the prize, hands down.) So in this chapter, I present a couple of patterns: One for leg warmers (aren't they just socks without feet?) and one for a pair of socks with a delicate lace pattern on the instep. Plus, I present two basic sock recipes: A chart for math nerds who like to figure things out on their own, and a formula for those who like things spelled out.

Simple Sock Formula and Socks By the Numbers, Plus a Chart for Kicks

Whether or not you like to work socks with lots of fancy stitchwork, there are times, especially when you have self-patterning or variegated yarn on hand, that you'll want to knit a pair of simple socks that will show off the beauty of the yarn. For this kind of sock, you don't really need a pattern. All you need are the tools to knit them: either a set of double-pointed needles or a circular needle or two, your yarn, and this basic recipe.

1. Make a gauge swatch and cast on enough stitches to fit around your foot in a multiple of even stitches for a 1x1 rib or a multiple of 4 for 2x2 rib. Work in the round, with the stitches divided among three double-pointed needles (dpn) with one-half of the stitches on one needle (these will become the heel stitches) and the other half divided onto the other two needles. If you knit with circulars, you'll have half on one and half on another. The ribbing is usually an inch or two long unless you decide to work the entire cuff in rib, which I do all the time. On a plain sock, the cuff is usually all Stockinette stitch and approximately 4 inches long.

2. Once the cuff is the desired length, place the instep stitches on hold by simply allowing them to stay on their needle(s), unworked.

3. Work the heel stitches flat as follows for 2 to 2½" or 2 rows less than the total number of heel stitches. So, if you have 30 stitches on your heel (for a 60-stitch sock), you'll work 28 rows for the heel. My favorite way to work them is:

Row 1 (WS): Slip 1, purl to end.

Row 2: *Slip 1, k1; repeat from * to end.

4. When the heel is complete, you'll end on a RS row, and then it is time to "turn the heel." This means you will work short rows to create a "cup" for your heel. In order to do this, with the WS facing, simply slip the first stitch and then purl to 2 stitches past the center of the row, p2tog, p1, turn. Then, with RS facing, slip 1, k5, ssk, k1, turn. You will notice that there will be a small gap between working stitches (the stitches you have just worked across), heel turn stitches (the p2tog or ssk and the following p1 or k1), and unworked heel stitches (the stitches on the other side of the p2tog, p1 and the ssk, k1 that you haven't gotten

The Edith Socks (page 130) are based on
the Simple Sock Formula with a pretty
lace panel thrown on the instep.

to yet). On the next row, slip 1, purl to 1 stitch before the gap, p2tog (the 2 stitches on either side of the gap), p1, turn. The following row is a RS row, so you will slip 1, knit to 1 stitch before the gap, ssk (the 2 stitches on either side of the gap), k1, turn. Repeat the last two rows, working one additional knit or purl stitch after the slip 1 until all side stitches are worked, ending with a RS row. Depending on how many stitches you began with for your heel, you may not be able to work the final p1 or k1 after the final decreases; don't worry about it. You will have reduced the number of stitches on the heel flap by about half, but you will make up for it later when you pick up gusset stitches. If, for some reason you haven't finished with a RS row, don't worry. Just turn your work and knit across.

5. For the gusset, using the needle you've been working with, pick up and knit stitches from the heel edges, one for every slipped stitch. Then, using another needle, knit across the instep stitches that you set aside earlier.

Using another needle, pick up stitches along the other side of the heel, again, one for every slipped stitch or half the number of rows you knit for the heel; with this same needle, knit to halfway across the heel. Place your beginning-of-round marker here. Knit one round. Next, continuing to knit in rounds, you will being decreasing before and after the instep stitches. But first take a look at your stitches and orient yourself. Your heel and side gusset stitches should be on two needles (if knitting on dpns) and the instep stitches should have their own needle. If working with circular needles, you probably have your favorite way of doing it, but generally speaking, most people have the instep stitches on one and all the other stitches on another.

6. Decrease Round: Knit to 3 stitches before the instep, k2tog, k1, work across the instep stitches to the end of the instep needle, k1, ssk, knit to the end. Work one plain round. Continue in this manner, working one plain round

SO WHAT MAKES KNITTING SOCKS SO SATISFYING?

Once you've knit a pair of socks or two and worn them around the house, you'll see why sock knitting can be so addictive. But to entice you to try it out, here are a few wonderful things about sock knitting:

✦ They are immensely portable. You can knit them on a rooftop, or in a car (as long as you're not the one driving), or really just about anywhere!

✦ You need only one, or sometimes two, small skeins of sock yarn to complete a pair.

✦ The sock yarn that's available is so fun and varied and exquisite: from hand-painted yarns from all over the world to special yarn that looks just like Fair Isle when you knit it up (It's magic! It does the work for you!).

✦ There are myriad tools and accessories available to the sock knitter: Blocking tools shaped like cute little socks; needles made of specialty woods especially for sock knitters; semitransparent shoes to show off your completed socks, and hundreds, if not thousands, of patterns to choose from.

✦ You can make them long or short, lacy and ornate, or plain and simple.

✦ You can knit socks a million different ways. Here are a few of my favorites: One at a time in the round on two circular needles, double-pointed needles, or on one super-short circular that is so small in circumference it won't distort your sock; two at a time on two circular needles; either one at a time or two at a time on one long circular needle using the "Magic Loop" technique; or one inside the other on double-pointed needles, à la "double-knitting" (especially if you like to show off).

in between decrease rounds, until you have an equal number of instep and heel stitches, or the original number of cast-on stitches. Then, continue working the foot of the sock in rounds until you have reached the desired length minus about 1 ½" for a children's sock and 2" for an adult sock.

7. Now you can decrease for the toe. A banded toe is one of the simplest and straightforward ways to work the toe. Make sure that you have instep stitches on one needle and the bottom of the foot stitches on the other two (or one if using circulars).

8. Decrease Round: K1, k2tog, work to 3 stitches before last instep stitch, ssk, k1, k1, k2tog, knit to the last 3 stitches, ssk, k1. Work one plain round. Continue decreasing in this manner and working one plain round every other round until you have 8 to 10 stitches left. Graft the remaining stitches together using Kitchener stitch (see Special Techniques on page 138).

Socks by the Numbers

Using this simple set of calculations, you can knit socks without a pattern. What's more, it's super easy to remember. So, if you're on the go and without a pattern, no problem!

Gauge (stitches per inch): _____

Foot circumference: _____

Stitches to cast on = Stitches per inch
x Foot circumference: _____ _____

Adjust stitches to cast on correct multiple for ribbing: _____ (Adj CO)

Heel stitches = Adj CO ÷ 2: _____

Rows for Heel length = (Heel stitches ÷ 2) – 2: _____

Turning Heel Flap stitches (number of stitches to purl before beginning heel turning) = (Heel stitches ÷ 2) + 2 = _____

Stitches to pick up for Gusset on each side = Heel rows ÷ 2 = _____

CHART FOR NON-MATH GEEKS

Use the chart below to determine the number of stitches you will need to work at the key stages of basic sock-making (cast-on, heel turning, and gusset). To get started, make a gauge swatch with the yarn you want to use and multiply the stitches per inch by your foot circumference. Look for the closest cast-on to that number in the first row, and use the corresponding numbers in the column to guide your sock knitting from there.

STITCHES TO CAST ON	44	48	52	56	60	64	68	72
STITCHES TO WORK FOR HEEL	22	24	26	28	30	32	34	36
ROWS TO WORK FOR HEEL	20	22	24	26	28	30	32	34
STITCHES TO WORK BEFORE TURN	13	14	15	16	17	18	19	20
STITCHES PICKED UP ALONG EACH GUSSET	11	12	13	14	15	16	17	18

CUFFED TEMARI GLOVES

I was yarn shopping with my friend Olga when I realized that one of my favorite yarns—Koigu KPPPM—in my favorite colorway comes in two weights: a fingering weight and a heavier weight. I originally had the idea of combining these two weights into cuffed gloves in the same colorway, but Olga suggested that I go with a contrasting color instead. And she was right: An allover variegated colorway was just too much. After I bought the yarn, we went next door to a button shop and bought these fabulous Bakelite vintage buttons that remind me of Temari balls, which I love to stitch (hence the name).

PATTERN FEATURES
Provisional cast-on, picking up and knitting, simple shaping.

SIZES
Medium (Large)

FINISHED MEASUREMENTS
7 ½ (8 ½)" hand circumference

YARN
Koigu Painter's Palette Premium Merino (KPPPM) (100% merino wool; 175 yards / 50 grams): 2 hanks #P118L (MC)

Koigu Wool Designs Kersti Merino Crepe (100% merino wool; 114 yards / 50 grams): 2 hanks #K2151 (A)

NEEDLES
One set of five double-pointed needles (dpn) size US 3 (3.25 mm)

One set of five double-pointed needles size US 5 (3.75 mm)

Change needle size if necessary to obtain correct gauge.

NOTIONS
Stitch marker; waste yarn; four ½" buttons

GAUGE
28 sts and 36 rnds = 4" (10 cm) in Stockinette stitch (St st), using smaller needles and MC

17 sts and 26 rows = 4" (10 cm) in Blanket Rib, using larger needles and A

STITCH PATTERNS

1x1 Rib

(multiple of 2 sts; 1-rnd repeat)

All Rnds: *K1, p1; repeat from * to end.

Blanket Rib

(multiple of 2 sts + 1; 2-row repeat)

Row 1 (WS): *K1-f/b; repeat from * to end (number of sts is doubled).

Row 2: K2tog, *p2tog, k2tog; repeat from * to end (original st count is restored).

Repeat Rows 1 and 2 for Blanket Rib.

NOTE

The Glove is begun with a Provisional CO at the Wrist (see Special Techniques, page 138), then worked through the Fingers. The Cuff is picked up from the Provisional CO and worked in the opposite direction.

WRIST

Note: After the initial Provisional CO, use Backward Loop CO for any other COs in this pattern (see Special Techniques, page 138). Using smaller needles, waste yarn, and Provisional CO, CO 52 (58) sts. Join for working in the rnd, being careful not to twist sts; pm for beginning of rnd. Change to MC; knit 1 rnd. Change to 1x1 Rib; work even for 3". Knit 1 rnd, increase 1 st at end of rnd—53 (59) sts.

Shape Thumb

Next Rnd: Continuing in St st (knit every rnd), work 26 (29) sts, pm, M1-l, k1, M1-r, work to end—55 (61) sts. Knit 2 rnds.

Increase Rnd: Work to marker, sm, M1-l, knit to next marker, M1-r, work to end—57 (63) sts.

Repeat Increase Rnd every 3 rnds 6 (9) times—69 (81) sts.

Next Rnd: Work to marker, transfer next 17 (23) sts to waste yarn for Thumb, removing markers, CO 1 st, knit to end—53 (59) sts.

HAND

Next Rnd: Continuing in St st, work even until piece measures 4 (4½)" from end of ribbing.

FINGERS

Little Finger

Next Rnd: K6 (7), transfer next 42 (46) sts to waste yarn, CO 1 (2) st(s) over gap, knit to end—12 (15) sts. Rearrange sts among 3 dpns. Join for working in the rnd; pm for beginning of rnd. Work even in St st until piece is long enough to cover finger [approximately 2 (2½)"].

Decrease Rnd: *K2tog; repeat from * to end of rnd, ending k3tog if there is an odd number of sts—6 (7) sts remain. Cut yarn, leaving a 12" tail; thread through remaining sts, pull tight and fasten off.

Upper Hand

Transfer sts from waste yarn to dpns. Rejoin MC at Little Finger, pick up and knit 2 sts at base of Little Finger, knit to end—44 (48) sts. Join for working in the rnd; pm for beginning of rnd. Knit 2 rnds.

Ring Finger

Next Rnd: K8, place next 28 (32) sts on waste yarn, CO 1 (2) st(s) over gap, knit to end—17 (18) sts. Rearrange sts among 3 dpns. Join for working in the rnd; pm for beginning of rnd. Work even in St st until piece is long enough to cover finger [approximately 2¼ (2¾)"]. Complete as for Little Finger.

Middle Finger

Next Rnd: Transfer first and last 7 (8) sts from waste yarn to dpns. Rejoin yarn between Middle and Ringer Fingers, pick up and knit 1 (2) st(s) from sts CO for Ring Finger, k7 (8), CO 1 (2) st(s) over gap, knit to end—16 (20) sts. Rearrange sts among 3 dpns. Join for working in the rnd; pm for beginning of rnd. Work even in St st until piece is long enough to cover finger [approximately 2 ½ (3)"]. Complete as for Little Finger.

Index Finger

Transfer remaining 14 (16) sts from waste yarn to dpns. Rejoin yarn between Index and Middle Fingers, pick up and knit 1 (2) st(s) from sts CO for Middle Finger, k7 (8)—15 (18) sts. Rearrange sts among 3 dpns. Join for working in the rnd; pm for beginning of rnd. Work even in St st until piece is long enough to cover finger [approximately 2 ¼ (2 ¾)"]. Complete as for Little Finger.

Thumb

Transfer sts from waste yarn to dpns. Rejoin yarn. Pick up and knit 1 st from st CO for gap, knit to end—18 sts. Rearrange sts among 3 dpns. Join for working in the rnd; pm for beginning of rnd. Work even in St st until piece is long enough to cover thumb [approximately 1 ¼ (1 ¾)"]. Complete as for Little Finger.

CUFF

Place marker between 2 center CO sts on Little Finger side of Glove. Carefully unravel Provisional CO and place sts on smaller dpns, with beginning of row between marked center sts. With RS facing, join A at beginning of row and, using larger dpns, CO 9 sts, purl to end, CO 9 sts—70 (76) sts. Knit 1 row, decrease 25 (29) sts between CO sts—45 (47) sts remain. *Note: When Cuff is completed, it will be folded over so that RS of Cuff will face RS of Wrist; original WS of Cuff will become new RS.*

Set-Up Row (RS): K1, *p1, k1; repeat from * to end.

Next Row: Change to Blanket Rib; work even until Cuff measures 3 ¼" from beginning, ending with Row 2 of pattern. BO all sts in 1x1 Rib, beginning with a purl st.

FINISHING

Using yarn tails, close gaps between Fingers. Sew buttons to Cuffs (see photo on page 114), sewing through both layers.

MAKE IT YOUR OWN

These gloves have ribbing beneath the cuffs, so if you want to make yours without cuffs, just use this pattern as a basic glove pattern and skip the cuff instructions at the end. You can also use a furry yarn for the cuffs instead of a smooth yarn for a bold, wintry statement.

DAFFODIL MITTS

These flouncy fingerless mitts are perfect for wearing in cold offices so you can answer the phone or type without losing dexterity. Or you can wear them in the springtime when you need just a little extra warmth and a splash of color. The mitts start out with a provisional cast-on and the ruffle is worked downward; then, the provisional stitches are placed back on the needles and the remainder is worked up to the fingertips.

PATTERN FEATURES
Provisional cast-on, simple stitch pattern, simple shaping.

SIZES

Youth Large/Women's X-Small (Women's Medium)

FINISHED MEASUREMENTS

6 (7)" hand circumference

5 (6)" wrist circumference

YARN

Scout's Swag 100% Superwash Wool Fingering (100% superwash merino wool; 400 yards / 50 grams): 1 hank Narcissus. *Note: You may substitute any fingering weight yarn that knits up at the gauge given here.*

NEEDLES

One set of five double-pointed needles (dpn) size US 2 (2.75 mm)

Change needle size if necessary to obtain correct gauge.

NOTIONS

Stitch markers; waste yarn

GAUGE

32 sts and 46 rnds = 4" (10 cm) in Stockinette stitch (St st)

STITCH PATTERNS

Openwork Rib
(multiple of 4 sts; 4-rnd repeat)

Rnds 1-3: *K2, p2; repeat from * to end.

Rnd 4: *Yo, ssk, p2; repeat from * to end.

Spiral Ruffle
(begins with multiple of 4 sts; 14 rnds)

Rnd 1: *K4, yo; repeat from * to end.

Rnd 2 and all Even-Numbered Rnds: Knit.

Rnd 3: *K5, yo; repeat from * to end.

Rnd 5: *K6, yo; repeat from * to end.

Rnds 7, 9, 11, and 13: Continue as established, knitting 1 more st between each yo on each rnd.

Rnd 14: Knit.

NOTE

These Mitts are worked in two pieces. The Wrist and Ruffle are worked from the wrist down, using a Provisional CO, from which you pick up stitches later and work from the wrist up to the Hand. Using a Provisional CO is optional; if you would prefer not to use one, use a cast-on of your choice, knit one row, then work the Wrist and Ruffle instructions, beginning after the CO. When you are ready to work the Hand, simply pick up the required stitches from the CO edge and work the Hand instructions.

WRIST AND RUFFLE

Using waste yarn and Provisional CO (see Special Techniques, page 138), CO 40 (48) sts. Join for working in the rnd, being careful not to twist sts; pm for beginning of rnd. Knit 1 rnd. Begin Openwork Rib; work Rnds 1–4 three times, then Rnds 1-3 once.

Shape Ruffle

Next Rnd: Change to Spiral Ruffle; work even for 14 rnds—110 (132) sts. Purl 1 rnd. Knit 1 rnd. Purl 1 rnd. BO all sts knitwise.

HAND

With RS of Wrist and Ruffle facing, carefully unravel Provisional CO and place sts onto 3 dpns. Join for working in the rnd; pm for beginning of rnd. Begin St st (knit every rnd); work even until piece measures 1" from ribbing, increase 8 sts evenly around—48 (56) sts. Work even until piece measures 3 ½ (4)" from ribbing.

Thumb Opening

Next Rnd: Change to waste yarn and k10 (14), slip these 10 (14) sts back to left-hand needle, change to working yarn, knit these 10 (14) sts again, knit to end. Work even until piece measures 1 ½" from Thumb Opening. Change to Openwork Rib; work Rnds 1–4 three times, then Rnds 1–3 once. BO all sts in pattern.

Thumb

Carefully remove waste yarn from Thumb sts and place top 10 (14) and bottom 10 (14) sts onto 2 dpns. Rejoin yarn to bottom sts, pick up and knit 1 st, knit across bottom sts, pick up and knit 1 st, knit across top sts—22 (30) sts. Redistribute sts among 3 dpns. Join for working in the rnd; pm for beginning of rnd. Begin St st; work even for 8 rnds.

Next Rnd: [K2tog, k9 (13)] twice—20 (28) sts remain. Change to Openwork Rib; work Rnds 1–4 once, then Rnds 1–3 once. BO all sts in pattern.

FINISHING

Block as desired.

MAKE IT YOUR OWN

If you have enough yarn, you can turn your mitt into a closed mitten on the fly. When you have worked approximately 4 ½ (5 ½)" of Stockinette, or 1 ½ (1 ¾)" less than the desired length, shape the top as follows: On the next round, *K10 (K12), k2tog around, then knit a plain round. Next, decrease 4 stitches by working one fewer knit stitch between decreases in this manner every other round until there are 20 (24) stitches left. Then, on every round decrease in the same manner until there are 8 stitches left. Cut the yarn, thread tail through the stitches, and cinch; fasten to the wrong side. Take a look at the Dartmoor Mittens on page 122 for extra guidance on how to shape mittens this way. For instructions on how to work a closed thumb, read the "Afterthought" Thumb Formula on page 109.

SIZES

Small (Medium, Large)

FINISHED MEASUREMENTS

Approximately 6 ½ (7 ½, 8 ½)" hand circumference

YARN

Blue Sky Alpacas Worsted Hand Dyes (50% alpaca / 50% merino; 100 yards / 100 grams): 3 (4, 4) hanks #2000 Red

NEEDLES

One set of five double-pointed needles (dpn) size US 9 (5.5 mm)

Change needle size if necessary to obtain correct gauge.

NOTIONS

Stitch markers in 2 colors; waste yarn

GAUGE

16 sts and 29 rows = 4" (10 cm) in Stockinette stitch (St st)

DARTMOOR MITTENS

My girlfriend from Alaska says she always likes big mittens like these because she can layer thin gloves underneath for extra warmth. And really, with the eyelets running up the backside of the mittens, wouldn't these look great with gloves in a contrasting color beneath? Whether for warmth or fashion, these mittens offer a great opportunity to play with layers.

STITCH PATTERN

Horseshoe Lace

Note: You may work pattern from text or Chart.
(multiple of 10 sts; 8-rnd repeat)

Rnd 1: *Yo, k3, sk2p, k3, yo, k1; repeat from * to end.

Rnd 2 and all Even-Numbered Rnds: Knit.

Rnd 3: *K1, yo, k2, sk2p, k2, yo, k2; repeat from * to end.

Rnd 5: *K2, yo, k1, sk2p, k1, yo, k3; repeat from * to end.

Rnd 7: *K3, yo, sk2p, yo, k4; repeat from * to end.

Rnd 8: Knit.

Repeat Rnds 1–8 for Horseshoe Lace.

RIGHT MITTEN

Cuff

CO 30 (40, 40) sts. Divide sts among 4 needles. Join for working in the rnd, being careful not to twist sts; pm for beginning of rnd. Begin Horseshoe Lace; work Rnds 1–8 four (5, 5) times, then Rnds 1–7 once.

Thumb Gusset

Rnd 1: Continue Horseshoe Lace across 10 sts, pm color A (same color as beginning-of-rnd marker), knit to end, decreasing 3 (9, 5) sts evenly to end—27 (31, 35) sts remain.

Rnd 2: Work to marker, sm, k3 (5, 7), pm color B, M1-l, k1, M1-r, pm color B, knit to end—29 (33, 37) sts.

Rnd 3: Work to marker, sm, knit to end.

Rnd 4: Increase 2 sts this rnd, then every 3 rnds 2 (3, 4) times, as follows: Work to marker, sm, M1-l, knit to marker, M1-r, sm, knit to end—35 (41, 47) sts.

Next Rnd: Work to first color B marker, transfer next 9 (11, 13) sts to waste yarn for Thumb, removing markers, CO 1 st using Backward Loop CO (see Special Techniques, page 138), knit to end—27 (31, 35) sts remain.

Hand

Next Rnd: Continuing to work Horseshoe Lace between color A markers as established, and St st on remaining

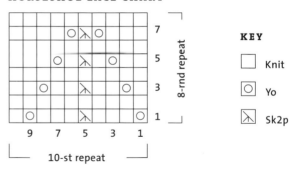

HORSESHOE LACE CHART

KEY

▢ Knit

⊙ Yo

⋌ Sk2p

8-rnd repeat

10-st repeat

sts; work even until piece reaches top of little finger, approximately 4 (5, 5½)" from end of Thumb Gusset, or to 1¼ (1½, 1¾)" less than desired length, ending with Rnd 7 of Horseshoe Lace. Knit 1 rnd, decrease 3 sts evenly—24 (28, 32) sts remain.

Shape Mitten Top

Decrease Rnd: *K4 (5, 6), k2tog; repeat from * to end—20 (24, 28) sts remain. Knit 1 rnd.

Working 1 fewer st before each k2tog on each decrease rnd, decrease 4 sts this rnd, every other rnd 0 (1, 2) time(s), then every rnd 3 (3, 2) times—4 (4, 8) sts remain. Cut yarn, leaving a 12" tail; thread through remaining sts, pull tight and fasten off.

Thumb

Transfer sts from waste yarn to dpns. Rejoin yarn. Pick up and knit 1 st from st CO for gap, knit to end—10 (12, 14) sts. Rearrange sts among 3 dpns. Join for working in the rnd; pm for beginning of rnd. Work even in St st until piece is long enough to cover thumb [approximately 1¼ (1½, 2)"].

Shape Thumb

Decrease Rnd: [K2tog, k1 (2, 3)] twice, k2tog, k2—7 (9, 11) sts remain. Knit 1 rnd.

Working 1 fewer st after each k2tog on each decrease rnd, decrease 3 sts this rnd, then every other rnd 0 (0, 1) time(s)—4 (6, 5) sts remain. Cut yarn, leaving a 12" tail; thread through remaining sts, pull tight, and fasten off.

LEFT MITTEN

Work as for Right Mitten to Thumb Gusset.

Thumb Gusset

Rnd 1: Work Horseshoe Lace across 10 sts, pm color A (same color as beginning-of-rnd marker), knit to end, decrease 3 (9, 5) sts evenly to end—27 (31, 35) sts remain.

Rnd 2: Work to marker, sm, k13 (15, 17), pm color B, M1-l, k1, M1-r, pm color B, knit to end—29 (33, 37) sts. Complete as for Right Mitten.

FINISHING

Block as desired.

MAKE IT YOUR OWN

If you want a fingerless version, it's easy to make the variation shown at right. After casting on as directed, work just two repeats of the Horseshoe Lace, then Rounds 1–7 again, before starting the thumb gusset. Once all gusset stitches have been added, place the thumb stitches on hold as directed and continue the lace portion in between the markers until the glove reaches your knuckles. After that, work 1x1 rib for approximately 1 inch and bind off in pattern. To make the thumbs, place the stitches onto double-pointed needles and pick up 1 stitch, knitting over the gap. After that, knit two plain Stockinette rounds, then work 1x1 rib for the same number of rounds as for the ribbing at the fingers. For a warmer version, substitute a bulky wool or replace the yarnovers with make-ones to close up the holes. This variation was worked in size Small with one hank of Blue Sky Alpacas Worsted Hand Dyes in #2021 Iris.

CANOODLE ARM WARMERS

I've spotted people around town with tube socks on their arms lately. No joke! I'm not sure if it's for fashion or because they got desperate during a cold snap, but I kind of like the look and thought I'd capture that old-skool tube-sock essence with these arm warmers. To make things even more fun, I added simple openings for thumbs so you can knit, type, text, or do whatever else you want without having to remove them.

SIZES

Youth (Women's Small, Medium, Large, X-Large, 2X-Large, 3X Large)

FINISHED MEASUREMENTS

7 ¾ (8 ¾, 9 ¾, 11, 12, 13 ¾, 15 ¾)" upper arm circumference

6 (7, 7 ¾, 7 ¾, 8, 8, 9)" hand circumference

YARN

Lorna's Laces Honor (70% baby alpaca / 30% silk; 275 yards / 100 grams): 1 (1, 1, 1, 1, 2, 2) hank(s) Violet (MC); 1 hank Island Blue (A). *Note: Since only a small amount of A is needed (no more than 15 grams), you may substitute any DK weight yarn that knits up at the gauge given here.*

NEEDLES

One set of five double-pointed needles (dpn) size US 5 (3.75 mm)

NOTIONS

Stitch marker

GAUGE

24 sts and 28 rnds = 4" (10 cm) in Stockinette stitch (St st) (knit every rnd)

28 sts and 28 rnds = 4" (10 cm) in 1x1 Rib

STITCH PATTERNS

1x1 Rib
(multiple of 2 sts; 1-rnd repeat)

All Rnds: *K1, p1; repeat from * to end.

Stripe Pattern
Working in St st, [work 4 rnds in A, 2 rnds in MC] twice, then 4 rnds in A.

ARM WARMERS (both alike)

Note: Arm Warmer is worked from the top down.

With MC, CO 46 (52, 58, 66, 72, 82, 94) sts. Join for working in the rnd, being careful not to twist sts; pm for beginning of rnd. Begin 1x1 Rib; work even for 1 ½ (1 ½, 1 ½, 1 ½, 1 ½, 2, 2)".

Next Rnd: Change to St st (knit every rnd); work even for 6 rnds.

Shape Arm and Work Stripes

Note: Arm shaping and stripes are worked at the same time; please read entire section through before beginning.

Next Rnd: Decrease 2 sts this rnd, then every 11 (15, 13, 7, 7, 5, 4) rnds 4 (4, 5, 9, 11, 16, 19) times, as follows: K1, k2tog, knit to 3 sts before marker, ssk, k1—36 (42, 46, 46, 48, 48, 54) sts remain. AT THE SAME TIME, when piece measures 8 (10, 10, 10, 11 ½, 11 ½, 11 ½)", work Stripe Pattern once. Work even until piece measures 11 ½ (14 ½, 14 ½, 14 ½, 16, 16, 16)" from the beginning, removing marker on last rnd; turn.

Thumb Opening

Row 1 (WS): K3, purl to last 3 sts, k3.

Row 2: Knit.

Repeat Rows 1 and 2 for 1 ½ (2, 2, 2, 2, 2, 2)", or to desired length for thumb opening, ending with Row 1.

Next Row (RS): Change to working in the rnd; pm for beginning of rnd. Work even in St st for 6 rnds. Change to 1x1 Rib; work even for 1". BO all sts in pattern.

FINISHING

Block as desired.

MAKE IT YOUR OWN

Instead of the stripes, insert some Fair Isle patterning anywhere you want—just plan ahead so those sections don't fall where you'll be shaping the arm. If the thumbhole isn't for you, it's easy to skip—after you have completed the shaping, try on the arm warmer to see where it lands, add ribbing to your desired length, then bind off, so it sits at your wrist instead.

FINISHED MEASUREMENTS

6 ¼ (7 ¾, 9 ½)" Foot circumference

6 ¾ (9 ½, 11)" Foot length from back
of Heel

6 (7, 7 ¾)" Leg length from Cuff to
base of Heel, with Cuff hemmed

YARN

Koigu Premium Merino (KPM) (100%
merino wool; 175 yards / 50 grams);
2 (2, 3) hanks #1113

NEEDLES

One set of five double-pointed
needles (dpn) size US 1 (2.25 mm)

One set of five double-pointed
needles size US 2 (2.75 mm)

Change needle size if necessary to
obtain correct gauge.

NOTIONS

Stitch markers

GAUGE

30 sts and 48 rows = 4" (10 cm) in
Stockinette st (St st), using larger
needles

EDITH SOCKS

When I designed these socks, I kept envisioning them on a
model wearing high heels, and when I told this to my editor,
Liana, she agreed. When our photo stylist, Mark, heard our
comments, he sighed: "Everyone's a stylist. Who do you
think you are . . . Edith Head?" And look who wound up
winning the debate. Regardless of how you wear them,
I hope you enjoy knitting them. These are worked from
the cuff down.

STITCH PATTERN

Lace Pattern

Note: You may work pattern from text or Chart.
(panel of 15 sts; 6-rnd repeat)

Rnd 1: P1, k1, p1, k2tog, k2, yo, k1, yo, k2, ssk, p1, k1, p1.

Rnds 2 and 4: P1, k1, p1, k9, p1, k1, p1.

Rnd 3: P1, k1, p1, k2tog, k1, yo, k3, yo, k1, ssk, p1, k1, p1.

Rnd 5: P1, k1, p1, k2tog, yo, k5, yo, ssk, p1, k1, p1.

Rnd 6: Repeat Rnd 2.

Repeat Rnds 1–6 for Lace Pattern.

CUFF

CO 48 (60, 72) sts. Divide sts among 3 needles [24-12-12 (30-15-15, 36-18-18)]. Join for working in the rnd, being careful not to twist sts; pm for beginning of rnd. Begin St st (knit every rnd); work even for 11 rnds.

Turning Rnd: *K2tog, yo; repeat from * to end.

Work even for 9 rnds.

Next Rnd: K1-f/b, knit to end—49 (61, 73) sts [25-12-12 (31-15-15, 37-18-18)].

LEG

Lace Pattern Set-Up Rnd: K5 (8, 11), pm, work Chart over 15 sts, pm, knit to end. Work even until piece measures 4 (4½, 5)" from Turning Rnd.

HEEL FLAP

Row 1 (WS): Turn. Slip 1, p23 (29, 35), working all 24 (30, 36) sts onto 1 needle for Heel Flap. Leave remaining 25 (31, 37) sts on needle for instep.

Row 2: *Slip 1, k1; repeat from * to end.

Repeat Rows 1 and 2 eleven (14, 15) times.

LACE PATTERN

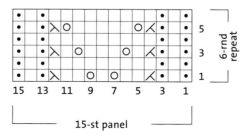

15-st panel · 6-rnd repeat

KEY

	Knit		Yo		Ssk
•	Purl		K2tog		

TURN HEEL

Row 1 (WS): Purl to last 10 (13, 16) sts, p2tog, p1, turn work.

Row 2: Slip 1, k5, ssk, k1, turn.

Row 3: Slip 1, purl to 1 st before gap, p2tog (the 2 sts on either side of gap), p1, turn.

Row 4: Slip 1 purlwise, knit to 1 st before gap, ssk (the 2 sts on either side of gap), k1, turn.

Repeat Rows 3 and 4 three (4, 6) times—14 (18, 20) sts remain; do not turn.

GUSSET

Next Row (RS): Needle 1: With Heel needle, pick up and knit 12 (15, 16) sts along left side of Heel Flap; **Needle 2:** Work across sts on instep needle as established; **Needle 3:** With spare needle, pick up and knit 12 (15, 16) sts along right side of Heel Flap, k7 (9, 10) from Needle 1. Join for working in the rnd; pm for beginning of rnd—63 (79, 89) sts [19-25-19 (24-31-24, 26-37-26)].

Decrease Rnd: Needle 1: Knit to last 3 sts, k2tog, k1; **Needle 2:** Work as established; **Needle 3:** K1, ssk, knit to end—61 (77, 87) sts remain [18-25-18 (23-31-23, 25-37-25)]. Work even for 1 rnd.

Repeat Decrease Rnd every other rnd 6 (8, 7) times—49 (61, 73) sts remain [12-25-12 (15-31-15, 18-37-18)].

FOOT

Work even in pattern as established until piece measures 5 ¼ (7 ¾, 8 ¾)", or to 1 ½ (1 ¾, 2 ¼)" less than desired length from back of Heel.

TOE

Decrease Rnd: Needle 1: Knit to last 3 sts, ssk, k1; **Needle 2:** K1, k2tog, knit to last 3 sts, removing markers and discontinuing Lace Pattern, ssk, k1; **Needle 3:** K1, k2tog, knit to end—45 (57, 69) sts remain. Knit 1 rnd.

Repeat Decrease Rnd every other rnd 7 (9, 12) times—17 (21, 21) sts remain [4-9-4 (5-11-5, 5-11-5)]. Knit 1 rnd.

Next Rnd: Needle 1: Knit to end; **Needle 2:** K2tog, knit to end; **Needle 3:** Knit to end—16 (20, 20) sts remain [4-8-4 (5-10-5, 5-10-5)]. Knit 1 rnd. Knit to end of Needle 1.

FINISHING

Break yarn, leaving long tail. Transfer sts from Needle 1 to Needle 3. Using Kitchener st (see Special Techniques, page 138), graft Toe sts.

Fold Cuff to WS at Turning Row and loosely sew to WS, being careful not to let sts show on RS.

Block as desired.

MAKE IT YOUR OWN

Since socks are basically a blank canvas, you can pretty much do anything you want to them. If you want to make a basic Stockinette-stitch sock, simply keep the stitch counts as they are. If you like, you can substitute the picot hem for regular ribbing and omit the center lace panel as well.

PATTERN FEATURES
Ribbing, simple stitch pattern,
twisted stitches.

SIZES

Youth (Women's Small/Medium,
Large)

FINISHED MEASUREMENTS

11 (13 ¼, 15 ½)" circumference

16 (19, 19)" long

YARN

Dream in Color Yarn Classy (100%
merino wool; 250 yards / 4 ounces):
2 hanks Lipstick Lava

NEEDLES

One set of five double-pointed
needles (dpn) size US 7 (4.5 mm)

Change needle size if necessary to
obtain correct gauge.

NOTIONS

Stitch marker

GAUGE

18 sts and 24 rows = 4" (10 cm) in
Spiral Columns Pattern

LIPSTICK LEG WARMERS

From the time my sister, Emily, was tiny, she took dance
classes and dreamt of becoming a dancer. These days,
she's a mom and a sound engineer in Hollywood, but I
always envision her pointing her toes under her desk at
work. Since the dancer in her was (and is) a big fan of leg
warmers, I asked for her advice on how these should turn
out. She said: "Long, slouchy, and stretchy enough to pull
over the feet in case it's cold." Then I asked her what color,
and she said "The color of our favorite lipstick."

STITCH PATTERNS

2x2 Rib
(multiple of 4 sts; 1-rnd repeat)

All Rnds: *K2, p2; repeat from * to end.

Spiral Columns Pattern
(multiple of 10 sts; 10-round repeat)

Rnds 1-4: *K6, p4; repeat from * to end.

Rnd 5: *K2, k2tog, k2, yo, p4; repeat from * to end.

Rnd 6: *K5, k1-tbl, p4; repeat from * to end.

Rnd 7: *K1, k2tog, k2, yo, k1, p4; repeat from * to end.

Rnd 8: K4, k1-tbl, k1, p4; repeat from * to end.

Rnd 9: K2tog, k2, yo, k2, p4; repeat from * to end.

Rnd 10: K3, k1-tbl, k2, p4; repeat from * to end

Repeat Rnds 1–10 for Spiral Columns Pattern.

LEG WARMER

CO 48 (60, 68) sts. Join for working in the rnd, being careful not to twist sts; pm for beginning of rnd. Begin 2x2 Rib; work even for 4", increase 2 (0, 2) sts on last rnd—50 (60, 70) sts.

SPIRAL COLUMNS PATTERN
(worked in the round)

KEY

☐	Knit
•	Purl
○	Yo
⟋	K2tog
℺	K1-tbl

Next Rnd: Change to Spiral Columns Pattern; work even until piece measures 12 (15, 15)" from the beginning, ending with Rnd 10 of Pattern.

Next Rnd: Change to 2x2 Rib, decrease 2 (0, 2) sts on first rnd; work even for 4"—48 (60, 68) sts remain. BO all sts in pattern.

MAKE IT YOUR OWN

If you want to omit the twisted stitches, go ahead and skip them! You can easily work 2x2 rib the whole way through if you so desire. If you want to insert a split by the heel so you get a "yoga-type" leg warmer with an opening for the heel, all you need to do is bind off half of the stitches on one round and then on the next round, cast on the same number of stitches at the same point, and then continue as usual.

SPECIAL TECHNIQUES

Backward Loop CO: Make a loop (using a slip knot) with the working yarn and place it on the right-hand needle (first st CO). *Wind yarn around thumb clockwise, insert right-hand needle into the front of the loop on thumb, remove thumb and tighten st on needle; repeat from * for remaining sts to be CO, or for casting on at the end of a row in progress.

Fringe: Using number of strands required in pattern, fold in half. With RS of piece facing, insert crochet hook just above edge to receive fringe, from back to front. Catch the folded strands of yarn with the hook and pull through work to form a loop. Insert ends of yarn through loop and pull to tighten.

I-Cord: Using a double-pointed needle, cast on or pick up the required number of sts; the working yarn will be at the left-hand side of the needle. *Transfer the needle with the sts to your left hand, bring the yarn around behind the work to the right-hand side. Using a second double-pointed needle, knit the sts from right to left, pulling the yarn from left to right for the first st; do not turn. Slide the sts to the opposite end of the needle; repeat from * until the I-Cord is the length desired. Note: After a few rows, the tubular shape will become apparent.

Kitchener Stitch: Using a blunt tapestry needle, thread a length of yarn approximately 4 times the length of the section to be joined. Hold the pieces to be joined wrong sides together, with the needles holding the sts parallel, both ends pointing to the right. Working from right to left, insert tapestry needle into first st on front needle as if to purl, pull yarn through, leaving st on needle; insert tapestry needle into first st on back needle as if to knit, pull yarn through, leaving st on needle; *insert tapestry needle into first st on front needle as if to knit, pull yarn through, removing st from needle; insert tapestry needle into next st on front needle as if to purl, pull yarn through, leaving st on needle; insert tapestry needle into first st on back needle as if to purl, pull yarn through, removing st from needle; insert tapestry needle into next st on back needle as if to knit, pull yarn through, leaving st on needle. Repeat from *, working 3 or 4 sts at a time, then go back and adjust tension to match the pieces being joined.

When 1 st remains on each needle, cut yarn and pass through last 2 sts to fasten off.

Pom-Pom: You can use a pom-pom maker or the following method: Cut two cardboard circles in the diameter of the pom-pom desired. Cut a 1"-diameter hole in the center of each circle. Cut a small wedge out of each circle to allow for wrapping yarn. Hold the circles together with the openings aligned. Wrap yarn around the circles until there is no room left in the center to wrap. Carefully cut yarn around outer edge of the cardboard circles. Using a 12" length of yarn, wrap around strands between the two circles and tie tightly. Slip the cardboard circles off the completed pom-pom; trim pom-pom, leaving the ends of the tie untrimmed. Using ends of tie, sew pom-pom to garment.

Provisional CO: Using waste yarn, CO the required number of sts; work in Stockinette st for 3 or 4 rows. Work 1 row with a thin, smooth yarn (crochet cotton or ravel cord used for machine knitting) as a separator; change to main yarn and continue as directed. When ready to work the live sts, pull out the separator row, placing the live sts on a spare needle.

Reading Charts: Unless otherwise specified in the instructions, when working straight, charts are read from right to left for RS rows, from left to right for WS rows. Row numbers are written at the beginning of each row. Numbers on the right indicate RS rows; numbers on the left indicate WS rows. When working circular, all rounds are read from right to left.

Stranded (Fair Isle) Colorwork Method: When more than one color is used per round, carry color(s) not in use loosely behind the WS of work. Be sure to secure all colors at beginning and end of rounds to prevent holes.

Three-Needle BO: Place the sts to be joined onto 2 same-size needles; hold the pieces to be joined with the RSs facing each other and the needles parallel, both pointing to the right. Holding both needles in your left hand, using working yarn and a third needle the same size or one size larger, insert the third needle into the first st on the front needle, then into the first st on the back needle; knit these 2 sts together; *knit the next st from each needle together

(2 sts on the right-hand needle); pass the first st over the second st to BO one st. Repeat from * until 1 st remains on the third needle; cut yarn and fasten off.

Working In the Round on Two Circular Needles: If your stitches are not already on 2 circular needles, divide them evenly (or as directed) between the needles. Hold the needles so that Needle 2 is in the back, with the working yarn at the right. Slide the stitches on Needle 2 to the cable of the needle; slide the stitches on Needle 1 to the tip of the needle closest to the working yarn. With the free end of Needle 1, work across the Needle 1 stitches as instructed, making sure to pull the yarn snug when working the first stitch, so that you do not have a gap between it and the last stitch on Needle 2. Once these stitches have been worked, slide the needle so that the stitches are on the cable of the needle. Turn the work so that Needle 1 is now in the back, with the working yarn at the right. Slide the stitches on Needle 2 to the tip closest to the working yarn. With the free end of Needle 2, work across the Needle 2 stitches as instructed, making sure to pull the yarn snug when working the first stitch. Continue working in this manner, always working with only one needle at a time, working the stitches on the needle with the free end of the same needle, and leaving the other needle hanging free.

HOW TO ADD BEADS USING A CROCHET HOOK

A lot of knitters are used to threading their beads onto the working yarn before starting their project, or buying yarn with the beads prestrung. There are times when you won't want to purchase prebeaded yarn, yet threading many small beads onto yarn beforehand can be a drag, and no one enjoys untangling beads and yarn that have spun and twirled up on themselves. Worse, sometimes the beads fuzz up the yarn while they hang as you work. Armed with a tiny crochet hook that will fit through the hole in the bead, you can skip the step of prethreading the beads and add beads to your knitting as you go.

1. Knit to the area where you want to place a bead.

2. Place a bead on your crochet hook.

3. With the bead still on the crochet hook, slip the stitch to receive the bead onto the crochet hook purlwise.

4. Slide the bead from the crochet hook onto the stitch so that the bead is sitting on the entire stitch.

5. Slide the stitch onto the right-hand needle with the yarn in back, using the crochet hook to hold the loop. You don't have to knit that stitch.

6. When you reach the stitch holding the bead on the next row (on either wrong side or right side), knit or purl the stitch as you would normally.

ABBREVIATIONS

BO: Bind off.

Circ: Circular

Cn: Cable needle

CO: Cast on

Dpn: Double-pointed needle(s)

K: Knit.

K1-f/b: Knit into front loop and back loop of same stitch to increase 1 stitch.

K1-tbl: Knit 1 stitch through the back loop, twisting the stitch.

K2tog: Knit 2 stitches together.

K3tog: Knit 3 stitches together.

M1 or M1-l (make 1-left slanting): With the tip of the left-hand needle inserted from front to back, lift the strand between the two needles onto the left-hand needle; knit the strand through the back loop to increase 1 stitch.

M1-r (make 1-right slanting): With the tip of the left-hand needle inserted from back to front, lift the strand between the two needles onto the left-hand needle; knit the strand through the front loop to increase 1 stitch.

P: Purl.

P2tog: Purl 2 stitches together.

Pm: Place marker.

Psso (pass slipped stitch over): Pass slipped stitch on right-hand needle over the stitches indicated in the instructions, as in binding off.

Rnd(s): Round(s)

RS: Right side

Sk2p (double decrease): Slip the next stitch knitwise to the right-hand needle, k2tog, pass the slipped stitch over the stitch from the k2tog.

Sm: Slip marker.

Ssk (slip, slip, knit): Slip the next 2 stitches to the right-hand needle one at a time as if to knit; return them back to the left-hand needle one at a time in their new orientation; knit them together through the back loop(s).

St(s): Stitch(es)

Tbl: Through the back loop

Tog: Together

WS: Wrong side

Wyib: With yarn in back

Wyif: With yarn in front

Yb: Yarn back

Yo: Yarnover (see Special Techniques, page 138)

YARN SOURCES

BERROCO, INC.
1 Tupperware Drive, Suite 4
North Smithfield, RI 02896
(401) 769-1212
www.berroco.com

BLUE SKY ALPACAS, INC.
P.O. Box 88
Cedar, MN 55011
(888) 460-8862
www.blueskyalpacas.com

BROWN SHEEP COMPANY, INC.
100662 County Road 16
Mitchell, NE 69357
(800) 826-9136
www.brownsheep.com

CRYSTAL PALACE YARNS
160 23rd Street
Richmond, CA 94804
www.straw.com

DREAM IN COLOR YARN, INC.
www.dreamincoloryarn.com

ELSEBETH LAVOLD YARNS
Distributor: Knitting Fever, Inc.

KNITTING FEVER, INC.
P.O. Box 336
315 Bayview Avenue
Amityville, NY 11701
(516) 546-3600
www.knittingfever.com

KOIGU WOOL DESIGNS
P.O. Box 158
Chatsworth, Ontario N0H IG0
Canada
(888) 765-WOOL
www.koigu.com

LORNA'S LACES
4229 North Honore Street
Chicago, IL 60613
(773) 935-3803
www.lornaslaces.net

MADELINETOSH
7515 Benbrook Parkway
Benbrook, TX 76126
(817) 249-3066
www.madelinetosh.com

MALABRIGO YARN
Wholesale Info:
(786) 866-6187
www.malabrigoyarn.com

MISTI INTERNATIONAL, INC.
P.O. Box 2532
Glen Ellyn, IL 60138
(888) 776-9276
www.mistialpaca.com

PAGEWOOD FARM
San Pedro, CA
(310) 403-7880
www.pagewoodfarm.com

PLYMOUTH YARN COMPANY, INC.
500 Lafayette Street
Bristol, PA 19007
(215) 788-0459
www.plymouthyarn.com

THE SANGUINE GRYPHON
www.sanguinegryphon.com

SCOUT'S SWAG
www.scoutsswag.com

SPUD & CHLOË
(see Blue Sky Alpacas, Inc.)
www.spudandchloe.com

TILLI TOMAS
(617) 524-3330
www.tillitomas.com

TWISTED SISTERS
www.twistedsistersknitting.com

ACKNOWLEDGMENTS

The thing I loved most about writing and designing for this book was rediscovering how fun, rewarding, sort of effortless, and without pressure accessory-knitting can be. After focusing on sweaters—my first love—over the last several years, I was reminded how pleasurable it is to make friends with a single skein of yarn. Two skeins. Maybe three. (In this collection, I never wrangled more than five skeins at once. Not that I don't love lots of yarn. Who doesn't?)

The stylist on the photo shoot, Mark Auria, had a wonderful reaction when he saw the knits for this book, and while he didn't say these words exactly, I could tell he was thinking, "Imagine how much fun it will be to accessorize the accessories!" I adore you, Mark. You have been a friend and true partner through and through. I love what you did with this collection of patterns—your fabulous fingerprint is on every single picture.

Liana Allday is my editor, and it turns out she grew up in a house a mile or two away from where I live and hung out at the same coffee shop for years, and we never knew each other. She went to the same high school as I did, too—although many years after me—and now she lives in New York and has a wonderful career in publishing. She edits my words and I love what she does. I think I have said it before, but she sort of channels my intention and turns my words into text that sounds more like me. Thank you, Liana, for all that you do. I know that you sometimes read something that seems wonky and you don't say a thing, but later, telepathically, you send me a message that causes me to wake up in the morning and correct whatever it is you thought wasn't quite right. Yes, we are practically telepathic, and a great team. I treasure our friendship and the way we work together. Thanks also to Melanie Falick, whose behind-the-scenes expertise has helped to form the Custom Knits series.

Joe Budd was on board as our photographer, and what can I say? Joe is the man with a camera you want on set. He's Zen. One day while we were shooting, I looked at his photos and remarked, "Hey Joe, all your shots have this beautiful light . . . an aura and a visceral feel. I can honestly see that each picture has your signature." And Joe, being the beautiful, wonderful spirit that he is, turned to me and said thank you in a way that you don't hear too often. Joe, I want to thank YOU. You captured the spirit and essence of the knits. You happily hopped on a boat in rough weather and choppy seas and managed to capture the model in an exquisite pose even though she was hanging on for dear life. (Which is more than I can say for myself—I was at home snug as a bug in a rug when that all went down, thank goodness.)

Red Dodge did the hair and makeup, and as you can see, Red has all the skills necessary and more to make the models even more beautiful. Red is one of those people, like Joe, who are great to have on set. Thank you, Red, for being with us on another book and making everyone look so spectacular. I also want to say thank you to Janet Rorschach, the food stylist on the shoot, for making such lovely and tasty "props." They were delish!

Thanks also to technical editor Sue McCain, who, like Liana Allday, reads my mind. Sue's ability to make my patterns clear and concise is a great gift. Also thank you to Therese Chynoweth for lending a second pair of eyes to the patterns in this book.

Tammy Reed helped me knit a couple items for the book, and they are beautiful. I was able to give her some yarn and some handwritten notes and she produced the garments perfectly!

Finally, I want to acknowledge my husband, Theron. What can I say? Through all these years, you've never complained about how, when I focus on a book, everything else around us (like our home and backyard garden) goes unnoticed by me. I will always be thankful for your kindness when I fret over a deadline or sit and knit in the corner for hours on end while you and Girlfriend watch movies beside me, keeping me company.

WENDY BERNARD is a knitwear designer based in Southern California. She is the author of *Custom Knits* and *Custom Knits 2* and is the creator of the popular blog Knit and Tonic (KnitandTonic.net). Her knitwear patterns have been published online by Knitty and Stitch Diva Studios, in the magazines *Interweave Knits* and *Knitscene*, in the books *No Sheep for You*, *Brave New Knits*, and *My Grandmother's Knitting* (STC), and in a DVD series teaching top-down knitting techniques. Her wholesale pattern line is available through Deep South Fibers.

JOE BUDD is a San Francisco-based photographer who has worked in advertising and print. His most recent clients include Levi's, Banana Republic, and Adidas.

MARK AURIA is a Los Angeles–based art director and wardrobe stylist who has worked in advertising, print, and television. His most recent clients include American and European fashion magazines and the corporations Zink, Pepsi, LG, and Apple.

ADDITIONAL CREDITS:

FIRST CAMERA ASSISTANT: Cameron Wong

CAMERA ASSISTANT: Theron Tan

HAIR/MAKEUP: Red Dodge

FOOD STYLIST: Janet Rorschach

PRODUCTION ASSISTANT: Miguel Cavazos

TALENT: Ana Ayora, Chelsea Chebo, Tyler Cook, Paul Galliano, Dominique Jane, Rhasaan Orange

MODELING AGENCY: Brand Model and Talent

CONTRIBUTING CLOTHING: Amy DeLeo for JuJuBead.com, Chris Dodge and Rebel Rouser Vintage, Positivitees.net